The Maharaja of Bikaner

The Maharaja of Bikaner
India
Hugh Purcell

First published in Great Britain in 2010 by
Haus Publishing Ltd
70 Cadogan Place
London SW1X 9AH
www.hauspublishing.com

A CIP catalogue record for this book
is available from the British Library

ISBN 978-1-905791-80-4

Series design by Susan Buchanan
Typeset in Sabon by MacGuru Ltd
Printed in Dubai by Oriental Press
Map by Martin Lubikowski, ML Design, London

Contents

Acknowledgements

I am grateful as usual to the staff of the Asian and Indian Studies Centre at the British Library. I am particularly grateful to Hanuwant Singh, the Secretary to the Maharaja Ganga Singh Trust in Bikaner, Rajasthan, and to the Librarian at the Archival Studies Centre at the Lallgarh Palace in Bikaner, Dalip Singh. They gave permission to my friend Prakash Dehta and my partner Margaret Percy to carry out the invaluable research for this book. I am fortunate in having such a persistent editor as Jaqueline Mitchell.

Prologue: 1919

On 15 November 1918, Ganga Singh, the 21st Maharaja of Bikaner, was at his palace in Rajasthan when he received a telegram from the Viceroy (*vice-roi*, literally 'in the place of the king'), King George V's representative and therefore the most senior British person in India. It said: 'As a result of communications between myself and London I am now in a position to ask Your Highness to proceed to England at once. It is absolutely essential that Your Highness should secure accommodation on the *Chindwara*, sailing on 23 instant from Bombay. Your Highness will be gratified to learn that the Prime Minister himself expressed a wish that you should go to London now. Precise method in which Your Highness' services will be asked has not yet been defined but I know Your Highness will understand the impossibility of getting matters clearly cut at the present juncture in the present stress.'[1]

This was the Maharaja's invitation to represent India at discussions in the Imperial War Cabinet and elsewhere about the peace settlement consequent upon the armistice with Germany, signed only a week before on 11 November. The status of an Indian delegation at the Peace Conference itself, due to begin at Paris in January, had not been decided. Indeed, it had not been decided whether India would be represented independently at all. This also applied to the Dominions of the British Empire, the name given to the member countries that governed themselves like Canada, Australia and South Africa. What had been decided was that India should be afforded the same status as a Dominion, although it was not a self-governing country. The fact that over one million Indian soldiers had fought for the British was considered reason enough to justify representation, if any were needed.

The fierce argument over representation called into question the very status of the Dominions. Were they nations or not? As the Prime Minister of Canada, Sir Robert Borden, wrote home to his wife: 'Canada is a nation that is not a nation and it is about time we altered it.'[2] What was their status *vis-à-vis* each other? Sir Maurice Hankey, Secretary to the British War Cabinet and then to the Peace Conference, said 'the Dominions are as jealous of each other as cats'.[3] The row rumbled across the continents to national parliaments well into December. At first the British government assumed the Prime Ministers of the Dominions would 'tag along to the Peace Conference as part of the British delegation'. This went down badly. Sir Robert Borden threatened to 'pack [his] trunks, return to Canada, summon Parliament, and put the whole thing before them'[4] unless Canada was given full representation. In the end the Prime Minister David Lloyd George gave way, and so did his two co-leaders in the Supreme War Council, Prime Minister Georges Clemenceau of France and President Woodrow Wilson of the United States. On 15 January 1919, 'the British Dominions and India' were classed as 'belligerent powers with special interests'. As such, their representatives were invited to take part in sessions of the Conference that specifically concerned them. Like the larger

Dominions, India was allowed two representatives, and here another contentious issue arose.

Lloyd George had already invited the Maharaja of Bikaner to represent the 600 Indian Princes. They formed a considerable power bloc because their states together covered about one-third of the land of India and one-fifth of the population. They were supposedly autonomous, and proud of the fact that they had sworn allegiance to the British Crown but not to the British government; a distinction of royal status. The remainder of the vast region – today divided into India, Pakistan, Bangladesh, Myanmar (Burma) and Sri Lanka – was British India in 1919, governed by a Secretary of State in London and a Viceroy in Delhi. The Viceroy, Lord Chelms ford, had asked Sir SP Sinha to represent British India, and in some ways he was an obvious choice. He was a Bengali lawyer with considerable political experience who already served on the Viceroy's Executive Council, the first Indian to do so. He, like Bikaner, had sat in the Imperial War Cabinet. Moreover, and this was what made his selection so obvious, Lloyd George was about to appoint him Under Secretary of State for India in his new Cabinet with a seat in the House of Lords. Thus, on 10 January 1919, Sir SP Sinha became the Lord Sinha of Raipur, the first Indian to be given a British peerage.

However, that left out of the delegation to Paris the Secretary of State for India, the Rt. Hon. Edwin Montagu, an ambitious politician who, unusually in that post, was dedicated to India. He was not pleased. He wrote to Lord Chelmsford: 'An attempt is made to invite only your nominees, but I claim they cannot represent you without me.'[5] He complained to Lloyd George, who gave in again. That meant three representatives in a delegation of two. What was to be done? Another form of words was required and the contemporary British history of the Peace Conference found one: 'India was represented by her Parliamentary spokesmen, the Secretary of State and Lord Sinha, with the co-operation of the Maharaja of Bikaner.'[6]

The three Indian delegates at the Paris Conference all shared the vision of an India governing itself, but under the might of the British Empire. The key word over which much constitutional hot air was expended was 'paramountcy', meaning pre-eminency or supremacy, yet there was obviously a paradox here, even a contradiction. As Sinha said, he believed India should achieve autonomy within the British Empire through 'gradual evolution and cautious progress',[7] but he could not think of a time when Britain would not be the paramount power in India.

Sinha, Bikaner and Montagu all believed the very presence of an Indian delegation at the Peace Conference with the same status as the Dominions was a huge step forward. Edwin Montagu wrote to Lord Chelmsford again: 'I wonder whether you ever have time to reflect upon the profound, irre-traceable [sic] changes that have been made in the Constitution of the British Empire in the last few months? We have gone – shall I say lightly? – into a series of decisions which put India so far as international affairs are concerned on a basis wholly inconsistent with the position of a subordinate country.'[8]

> 'We have gone – shall I say lightly? – into a series of decisions which put India so far as international affairs are concerned on a basis wholly inconsistent with the position of a subordinate country.'
> EDWIN MONTAGU, 1919

Lord Chelmsford did not share Montagu's excitement. He replied lugubriously: 'You set out the extraordinary development in India's constitutional position. I entirely agree with you, but I do not think it would be wise for you or me to count on gratitude or respect. Someone said to me the other day "India is grateful not for the past but for favours to come" and as I look back over the last three years and see the number of remedies I have made to supposed injustices, I despair, because these things are in no sense counted as righteousness but are forgotten and put aside.'[9]

What were these 'reforms' Montagu referred to? By a coincidence of timing, during the same few months Montagu and Sinha were at the Paris Peace Conference increasing the standing of India in an international forum, they were also steering through the British Parliament the Government of India Bill that would set up provincial legislatures in India empowering Indians to have more control over their own local affairs, an early step towards self-rule. This was why Lord Sinha had been appointed.

The first few months of 1919 were momentous times in the history of Indian independence. What happened in Paris and London was only part of the story. Far away from the chandeliers and champagne of these two capitals, in the stifling heat and poverty of a north Indian town, a tragedy took place that provoked the human rights lawyer and political activist Mohandas Gandhi to begin his demand for *swaraj*, or complete self-government for India. This was the Amritsar Massacre of April 1919. In an enclosed public area the size of Trafalgar Square, troops of the British Indian Army fired on a peaceful rally protesting against British rule. They killed or wounded nearly 2,000 civilians in a matter of minutes. In India this atrocity overwhelmed any goodwill the British government was earning with its Government of India Bill and by its advocacy of constitutional autonomy for India in Paris. It pushed to one side the pro-British reformers led by Montagu, Sinha and Bikaner, and gave centre stage to

MOHANDAS GANDHI (1869–1948)

Gandhi was surely the most extraordinary freedom fighter of the 20th century because he believed in transforming society morally as well as politically. True independence meant not just removing the British Raj, but replacing it with communities that were self-sufficient, simple and peaceful. He exemplified this in his own life by wearing home-spun cotton, eating a vegetarian diet, eschewing violence and extending love to all irrespective of race or religion.

Gandhi came from a Hindu family but he saw God everywhere and he spoke for all religious communities. His doctrine of *satyagraha* did not mean 'passive resistance' as a consequence of direct action, but literally, 'truth force'. He believed spiritual strength came from the rightness of the cause, sufficient to withstand prison and police beatings. He was revered like a god and his spiritual powers were invoked: 'O *Mahatma* ('great soul'), make my body non-violent' a passive resister might say as the blow of the *lathi* (police truncheon) hit his back.

Gandhi came from a middle-class trading family in Gujarat and first practised as a lawyer representing downtrodden Indians in South Africa. Yet he loved the life of the Indian village, and saw the peasants as his natural allies. This was why the Indian National Congress recognised him as indispensable: 'He is a man of commanding personality who inspires devotion in India's millions' said Jawaharlal Nehru. His philosophy offered a way forward that was neither the slow-moving constitutionalism of Bikaner and Sinha, nor the self-destructive terrorism of Bal Tilak. He was also a born showman and a shrewd politician.

Hence he overcame the might of the British Empire. One is bound to ask, nevertheless, whether his *satyagraha* would have been as effective against the totalitarian regimes of the age, Hitler's Nazism and Stalin's Communism.

Gandhi, a saint-like revolutionary who soon became known throughout India as the *mahatma* or 'great soul', the Father of the Nation. His vision was for *pura swaraj* (Hindi for 'complete independence') and now, outraged by the massacre in Amritsar, he set out on his path of *satyagraha* ('passive resistance') in order to achieve it.

The full significance of Amritsar did not register in Paris

at the time. The British Empire delegation had a more pressing question to answer. Come the signing of the Treaty of Versailles in June, who should sign first on behalf of India – Bikaner, the princely soldier, or Sinha, the Bengali politician? The King-Emperor, as George V was titled, was consulted over the telephone. According to Montagu, he 'expressed himself emphatically of the opinion that Bikaner's name should come first'.[10] This is not surprising, for King George and the Maharaja of Bikaner were friends. In fact Bikaner had been a most loyal ADC (honorary *aide de camp* or assistant) to King George since their first meeting in 1902 when the Maharaja had visited London for the coronation of Edward VII; then, of course, the future King George V was still Prince of Wales. On subsequent meetings, they indulged each other with shooting parties and gossip rather than talk of politics. King George then astonished Montagu by saying 'he was surprised to learn that Bikaner was not a British subject!'[11] This speaks well for Bikaner's loyalty to King George and his English accent – he prided himself in his knowledge of Edwardian slang – but less well for the King-Emperor's powers of observation.

> 'He is a figure out of the *Arabian Nights* with jewel-studded turban, an exceedingly handsome countenance and upright bearing.'
> FRANCES STEVENSON ON THE MAHARAJA OF BIKANER

In the end, Montagu and Bikaner signed the Treaty of Versailles and Sinha did not. A modest, self-effacing man who referred to himself as 'just a foot soldier of reform',[12] Sinha probably eschewed the limelight. The same could not be said of the Maharaja, an extrovert who enjoyed the many trappings of his rank. Lloyd George referred to him as a 'magnificent specimen of manhood' and Lloyd George's secretary and mistress Frances Stevenson was even more adulatory: 'He is a figure out of the *Arabian Nights* with jewel-studded turban, an exceedingly handsome countenance and upright bearing.' [13]

One wonders if that is why the artist Sir William Orpen, when painting his iconic picture *The Signing of the Peace* now hanging in the Imperial War Museum, London, stood him and Sir Edwin Montagu directly behind Lloyd George. There is the majestic Maharaja, placed centre-stage between two pillars with the light shining on him from the mirror behind. Yet probably the first reaction of many who gaze at this picture is to wonder what this exotic character, so conspicuous among the elderly Western statesmen, was doing at the Paris Peace Conference.

The young Maharaja Ganga Singh of Bikaner and his British Agent Sir Charles Bayley

Maharaja Ganga Singh sits with his council of Elders

I
The Life and the Land

The Maharaja of Bikaner is seated between the Viceroy and Vicereine of India,
Lord and Lady Curzon. 1902

1

The Maharaja of Bikaner and the Indian Princes

Ganga Singh, Maharaja of Bikaner, was born on 13 October 1880. When he was only seven he became the 21st ruler of the desert kingdom. The founder of the line, Rao Bika, belonged to the warrior clan of Rathores, whose patriotism and valour were already celebrated in Indian history. In 1465 he had marched north from Jodhpur with 600 soldiers, through a semi-arid, de-populated wasteland, and stopped at a village called Deshnok. Here lived a woman, Sri Karniji, who was worshipped as semi-divine. She announced to Rao Bika that 'your destiny is higher than your father's and many servants will touch your feet'.[1] So he built a fort, 'Bika's fort' and that became the town of Bikaner. By 1949, when all the kingdoms of the Rajput princes (for the Rathores were a branch of Rajputs who claimed to be the original Hindu warrior dynasty) were merged into the Union of Rajasthan, the state of Bikaner covered 23,000 square miles and was the sixth largest Indian princedom.

Until Ganga Singh built the famous Gang Canal in the 1920s, which transformed the state, it was a princedom with few attractions. On the edge of the forbidding Thar Desert, only sand dunes met the eye for vast stretches, the scorching sun making human and animal life a daily struggle against nature. The annual rainfall is only 11 inches. Until the reign of Ganga Singh's predecessor, Maharaja Dungar Singh (1872–87), no roads, schools or hospitals existed; the administration of the state was minimal save for keeping a large and untrained army that was employed to subdue rebel *thakurs*, the Rajput chiefs. Famines were frequent, decimating a population that on Ganga Singh's accession numbered just under one million.

Yet Bikaner had strategic importance. The caravan routes across the Thar Desert, carrying trade to and from the west coast, converged first on Rajgarh and then on the town of Bikaner itself, which is only 400 miles or so south-west of Delhi. Today, the Pakistan border bisects the Thar Desert, but in the days of Ganga Singh it was the border with another state of British India called Sind. To the north lay the warlike land of the Punjab through which enemies of India could march on Delhi. Impregnable forts guarded this border. Within the principality of Bikaner, the Rathore princes were frequently troubled by rebellious *thakurs*. So on the one hand, the great Mughals and subsequently the British needed alliances with the Rathores to protect Delhi. On the other hand, the Rathores needed alliances with the powers in Delhi to protect their kingdom. Ganga Singh followed family tradition by basing his reputation on royal alliances.

The Mughal dynasty dominated north India from Babur's victory near Delhi in 1526 to Aurangzeb's death in 1707. During this entire period all sixteen rulers of Bikaner, either at the head of their own troops or in command of an imperial army, fought for the Mughals, extending their power throughout the subcontinent, except the south. As a result, they were awarded vice-royalties, governorships and the hereditary title of Maharaja (*maha-raja* means literally 'great ruler'). The Bikaner dynasty grew with the Mughal dynasty and soon eclipsed the other Rajput states, and when the Mughal Empire disintegrated the state of Bikaner was also reduced to anarchy, though it was never conquered by another powerful dynasty rising to the south, the Marathas.

Then the British arrived. Reversing the axiom that trade follows the flag, the East India Company Army followed its merchants. In 1818 its Governor-General, the Marquess of Hastings, promised a treaty of 'perpetual friendship, alliance and unity of interests'[2] to Maharaja Surat Singh of Bikaner. This alliance became what Ganga Singh was later to call 'the Magna Carta of the Bikaner State',[3] so its wording needs to be looked at with care. It declared that the friends and enemies of one party were the friends and enemies of both. It established 'an absolute unity of interests'. In the short term, the East India Company Army easily defeated the *thakurs* and established security. In the longer term, the British Political Agent at the princely court made sure 'unity of interest' really meant the supremacy of British interest, and so it was throughout all the Indian princedoms that had similar treaties.

THE MUGHAL DYNASTY
The first Mughal ruler to come from Persia and conquer north India was Babur, who entered Delhi in 1526. His five descendants, ending with Aurangzeb who died in 1707, were larger than life, brilliant and vital rulers who claimed the blood of Genghis Khan and Timur flowed in their veins. Their monuments, like the tomb of the Taj Mahal in Agra and the private audience chamber, the Diwan-e-Khaas, in the Red Fort of Delhi with its inscription 'If there is paradise on earth it is here, it is here, it is here', are among the most beautiful in the world. The last Mughal Emperor, Bahadur Zafar II, was expelled by the British from Delhi in 1858 for his part in the great uprising.

In fact this was one of the causes of the Indian Mutiny, now called 'the First War of Independence' in India. In 1848 Governor-General Dalhousie passed the notorious 'law of lapse' which empowered the East India Company to take over a princedom if it found the heir to the throne unworthy to rule. Several leaders of the rebel army, including the heroic Rani of Jhansi, were heirs apparent who found their princedoms confiscated. The Mutiny broke out in 1857 and the so-called 'Devil's Wind' consumed the arid plains of north India with terrible fury – on both sides.

By no means all the Indian rulers joined the insurrection. Ganga Singh's role model was the 19th Maharaja of Bikaner, Sarda Singh, who stood firm with the British. It looked for a while as though the rebels, having captured Delhi, would march on the British capital of Calcutta. Those with a fearful disposition predicted the rebels in Delhi would be joined by the fierce tribesmen of the Punjab, only recently conquered by the East India Company Army in two costly wars. While other princes wavered, waiting to see which way the wind would blow, Sarda Singh instantly threw his lot in with the British. He personally marched his army to its northern border with the Punjab and occupied the town of Hassar, a strategic stronghold on the old road to Delhi. Under his command in the field, his well-drilled cavalry supported by a camel corps defeated the rebels in several battles.

THE INDIAN MUTINY (1857–8)
At the time this great uprising against the East India Company that ruled India on behalf of the British government was known as 'the Devil's Wind', because it consumed all in its path across the scorched plains of North India in an orgy of violence – by both sides. It was more than a 'mutiny', as the British call it, because it extended to the civil population. But it was less than a 'War of Indian Independence', as Indians call it, because it had no political aim except driving out the British, and it only affected the north of the country.

Without his timely action the revolt might well have spread to the Punjab and radically strengthened the rebel armies. Afterwards, the British were fulsome in their praise of Sarda Singh. The official dispatch put it in capitals: 'NO PRINCE IN RAJPUTANA SAVE BIKANER TOOK THE FIELD IN PERSON IN OUR FAVOUR WITHOUT HESITATION; BY HIS COURAGE AND EXAMPLE OF HIS LOYALTY HE CHECKED DISAFFECTION AND GAVE CONFIDENCE TO THE WAVERING.' [4] Queen Victoria herself, soon to assume the mantle of Empress of India, sent a *kharita* (a formal letter exchanged between rulers) which was presented at a *durbar* (a ceremonial gathering of princes): 'It is in such times that the true quality of friendship is tested. Her Majesty is deeply sensible of the loyalty and devotion displayed by Your Highness … '.[5]

The 19th Maharaja was a real prince in the genuine Indian tradition and the 21st Maharaja followed his example. Ninety-nine elephants filled Sarda Singh's stables and his military establishment was well beyond his means and needs in both size and grandeur. General Hervey visited him in about 1860 and described a scene that could have been reproduced as a British picture of the 'magnificent Orient': 'We reached the fort just as the Maharajah had emerged through its gateway, seated grandly in a state *peenus* or sedan chair, born by men in scarlet livery. This fine conveyance was emblazoned with designs of gold, and set around with deep gold fringes, a rich silk canopy covering it, reared at the corners upon shafts of gold. He was greeted by a salute from two cannons made of burnished brass, worked by his *golundaz*, or artillerymen. I observed that a large loaded pistol was placed by his side. His attire was the usual Rajpootanah long robe, the skirts thereof in the amplest of pleatings; a finely hilted dagger in his waistband, a handsomely sheathed sword held in his right hand, some diamond rings on his fingers, rich gold bracelets on his wrists, and a deep necklace of large pearls with a fine single emerald suspended at its centre, his tall head-gear being decorated with the diamond aigrette in the shape of the figure 6, peculiar to Rajpoot princes; and a superb diamond frontlet of a single stone, pendant over his forehead from the front part of his head-dress.'[6] If Lloyd George's secretary thought the 21st Maharaja of Bikaner was out of the *Arabian Nights*, then the pomp and display of the 19th would have attracted attention at the court of Queen Victoria herself.

After the Mutiny had been quelled in 1858, the British government pushed aside the East India Company and ruled India directly. Its vision became increasingly imperialistic at the expense of the autonomy of the princely states, but the British Empire won the loyalty of the princes by decreeing they owed allegiance not to the British Parliament but to the British Crown. Queen Victoria became Empress of India and the Indian princes bowed the knee to her or to her representative in India, the Viceroy. In their own kingdoms the princes were supposedly sovereign. The illusion was maintained by grand *durbars* with their Emperor or his Viceroy, and by the showering of titles and honours. In reality this was a semi-fiction. A good example of this was the accession to the throne of Bikaner by the young Ganga Singh.

In 1887 Maharaja Dungar Singh lay dying, without a son and heir. He sent a *kharita* to the Viceroy Lord Dufferin through the Political Agent in Bikaner, A P Thornton: 'I have according to my intention, adopted my brother, Ganga Singh, who will succeed me. I request that the Government of India may confirm the succession of my brother after my demise.'[7] The Viceroy confirmed the *kharita* and on 21 August Ganga

Singh was proclaimed the 21st Maharaja. Until he was 18, in 1898, a Council of Regency controlled the state of Bikaner. Its President was Sir Charles Bayley, the new Political Agent, for it was set up by the British government. Such was the extent of British control over supposedly sovereign princes in India.

By the time Maharaja Ganga Singh assumed power in 1898, the once-sovereign princes in alliance with the Crown had become 'chiefs under the suzerainty' of Britain. This quaint pseudo-feudal language was used by the Government of India to denote the new status. Other words from the same language crept into documents, like 'wardship' and 'allegiance'. When the Political Agent in Bikaner wrote to Ganga Singh in 1898 to confirm his assumption of power, the language may have been supercilious but it was certainly not archaic:

'My dear Maharaja,

I am directed to inform you that the Government of India have decided that Your Highness may now be entrusted with the management of your state, subject to certain limitations to be imposed for a time.

These limitations are:

(1) That no measures or acts taken or done by the Council of Regency during the minority may be altered or revised without the concurrence of the Political Resident.

(2) That the Political Resident's approval must be obtained before any important change is introduced

(3) That His Highness the Maharaja will not act against the Political Resident's advice in any important matter.

I am to ask you to send me a formal acceptance in writing of these limitations.

Yours sincerely

H A Vincent'[8]

Worse was to come when Lord Curzon became Viceroy the following year. His period in office was dubbed 'the climax of Empire', resonating with Elgar's 'Pomp and Circumstance' music, and dazzling with the Parade of Princes at the Delhi *durbar* in honour of King Edward VII in 1903 when bejewelled maharajas on magnificently-caparisoned elephants paid homage. He declared the princes were no longer 'the architectural adornments of the imperial edifice but the pillars that help to sustain the main roof'. At about the same time he also declared that 'the sovereignty of the Crown is everywhere unchallenged; it has itself laid down the limitations of its own prerogative'.[9] This meant it could override any existing treaties or rights. In other words, the princes were not sovereign, and to make that humiliatingly clear the Government of India instituted a scheme of prohibitions. Maharajas were not to call their sons princes; they were not supposed to 'reign' but only to 'rule'; their troops were not 'armies' but only 'forces'. The 's' word as in 'sovereign' was to be avoided unless it applied to the British Crown.

Curzon said he wanted the princes to be 'not relics but rulers, not puppets but living factors in the administration'.[10] What he meant was he conceded them power provided they accepted the 'paramountcy' of the Crown. In his interpretation of that archaic word, this justified his interference, even in the detail, of how they ran their states. From his early years as Maharaja, Ganga Singh objected to this. He accepted 'paramountcy' but questioned where the line should be drawn over his own autocracy. In fact his future reputation as a progressive politician seeking Indian autonomy may be traced back to the arguments he had with the Political Agent in Bikaner over his own autonomy.

The Regency sent young Ganga Singh to Mayo College in Ajmer when he was nine. This was the Eton of India, a Princes' College with a European staff who believed dogmatically what was good for Europeans was good for Indians. Its task was to educate young princes to rule, to inculcate loyalty to the British government and to persuade in the superiority of all things European. In the view of one teacher, this meant all things English – 'the speaking of faultless English, the playing of good cricket and the possession of good table manners'.[11] By all accounts it succeeded with Ganga Singh. He always won first prize for English. Gifted with a resonant voice, he loved oratory, both extemporaneous debate and recitation. His elocution was perfect. In later years, when he was regarded a leading speaker at international meetings in Europe, he had much to thank Mayo for. Although not an intellectual, he had a quick grasp of knowledge and a diligent approach to study. He left in 1895 when he was fourteen.

Then the Regency chose a personal tutor at Bikaner for him to develop his military skills, such as riding and shooting, and his understanding of government – British of course. Mr Brian Egerton soon won over his ward by his wholehearted dedication to the task in hand. The Maharaja remembered in an anecdote that says much about living conditions in this poor desert kingdom: *Sir Brian* [as he later became] *came here in the pleasant month of July* [this was a joke of course as the temperature would be in the mid 40s] *before the rains had broken. We were then living in the Fort, in that part of the old palace which had only recently been partly completed*

– minus electric light, minus electric fans, minus khas tattis [air coolers] *and minus water pipes; in short minus all modern conveniences. Colonel Tom ffrench-Mullen [sic], who was our doctor here, attempted to insist that he should not stay in the Fort as it was not fit for a European. His response was that his place was with his ward and he had to share his discomfort.*[12]

And Sir Brian remembered: 'While His Highness was assiduous at his studies, his activity was amazing. Riding and shooting before breakfast and study morning and afternoon, polo in the evening, and at a later date roller skating to finish up with, was an ordinary day's routine varied on holidays by a ride out eighteen miles to Gajner, shooting and pig-sticking there, and riding back in time for polo in the afternoon.'[13]

Photographs of the Maharaja at the time of his assumption of power in 1898 show a tall, slim young man with a self-consciously erect bearing. What catches the eye is his face: the pale skin, already slightly fleshy, adorned with a luxurious moustache curling up at the ends and above that always a sumptuous turban. He was something of a dandy. His recent biographer, Professor L S Rathore, claims in his private life he was 'a simple and unaffected gentleman' but his daily dressing routine gives a different impression: 'Every day, after a bath, for at least ten minutes, he set his moustache with a very fine elastic netting. One of his courtiers recorded: "After he had put on his clothes he would go to the room where his shoes were all in a row, and he would pick up a long pointer like you have in school. He would just touch one of the shoes with it, and that pair would be polished and brushed. Then in the lobby, there was his collection of walking sticks, and he would pick out one. Then a tray containing cigarette cases, one of which he would select. So he was very particular."'[14]

The Maharaja clearly thought that appearances mattered,

and that a public appearance was the opportunity for show-manship. When Curzon's successor, Lord Minto, paid his first visit in 1906, the Maharaja met him at the newly-built Bikaner station. Professor Rathore describes the scene: 'He was resplendent in brocaded silk and looking magnificent in rainbow hued breeches with jewelled *aigrette* [a tuft of long egret plumes worn on his turban]. The escorts, in gold and white uniform, were mounted on camels with crimson trap-pings decorated with necklaces of shells. Troops lined the road up to the palace, some dressed in chain armour with visors over their faces, silver bullock-carts drawn up in for-mation, with the horns of the bullocks encased in embossed silver; behind the troops the crowd made a riot of colour. As Lord Minto and the Maharaja drove by, the people chanted *khoma, khoma* – meaning, "Pardon mighty Lord".' [15]

When so much of British authority depended on display and hierarchy, the Maharaja of Bikaner was in his element. As Lord Curzon said on his visit in 1902, Ganga Singh 'could combine the merits of the East and the West in a single blend'.[16] The Maharaja added his own taste for the ceremo-nial richness and caste-consciousness of India to the imperial ostentation of the British. The wife of a later Viceroy (Lady Irwin, speaking in the 1930s) said Bikaner 'exalted snobbery to the realm of genius. One would not have taken him at first sight for an Indian Prince. He might have been a European diplomat of some distinction who spoke English and French perfectly and was clearly on easy terms with the great in London and Paris, as one could tell by his casual references to their Christian names.' [17] Bikaner acquired his style through the nature of India and the nurture of the Empire.

It would be wrong to consider the Maharaja of Bikaner a dilettante as well as a dandy. He was an enormously hard worker and a most effective ruler. In the desert landscape where the combination of heat and temperament can cause inertia, Bikaner got things done. No wonder Lord Curzon had a soft spot for him, for they were very similar. Beneath a liking for display and a keen sense of their own status, both possessed energy and a craving for efficiency. Bikaner's work routine was typical of him. His day began at eight o'clock when he would sit at the head of his office table. With a number of blue and red pencils of gigantic size on either side and surrounded by numerous stenographers and secretaries, he would pour over files and correct drafts. He worked until 11.30 a.m. when he retired for his religious observance and midday meal. Work began again at 2.30 p.m. with a procession of appointments: ministers, petitioners, delegations. At 4.30 p.m., when the weather was cooler, he would go on tours of inspection.[18]

Work continued in the evening. His daughter, Princess Shiv Kanwar, recalled: 'When my father used to come for dinner, sometimes we were allowed to sit there with him. He would have his pencils and chit-pads and while eating he would write with his left hand, making notes. We would sharpen his pencils, thinking that we were great office bearers.'[19] The Maharaja's day often ended with a visit to the court prostitutes, faithfully recorded by one of his staff: '10.00 p.m. went to the room of the prostitute from Gwalior, Mungu. Left at 11.30 p.m. He was kind to her and gave her 50 rupees.'[20]

In 1897, when the Maharaja was 17, the Regency Council chose for his bride the young Princess of Pratapgarh from south Rajasthan. The Maharaja's marriages were arranged for him, after due consultation with horologists and priests and, of course, due negotiation over the size of dowry. It is, however, difficult to write about the marriages of Ganga

Singh because his wives were all in *purdah* (literally 'curtain'), meaning they seldom appeared in mixed company outside the home. This was the custom among high-born Hindu ladies in that part of India and the Maharaja, despite his Western ways in Europe, was in India a traditionalist as befitted a great Rajput prince. No photographs exist of his wives, though in *The Desert Kingdom*[21] there is a revealing group photograph of the Baroda royal family taken in about 1930. It shows the Maharaja of Bikaner looking sternly straight ahead while the young Maharani Chimra Bai, a firm believer in emancipation, squeezes next to him. Wearing a Western dress that ends below the knee, and with her head and face uncovered, she looks coquettish in the circumstances.

The Princess of Pratapgarh gave birth to three children, of whom the first died after a few hours. Princess Chand Kanwar survived childhood but died of tuberculosis during the First World War. Third born in 1902 was Prince Sadul Singh, son and heir, who succeeded to the throne in 1943. Photographs show a proud but no doubt distant father posing with his two young children, weighed down with finery.

The most influential woman in the Maharaja's life was his mother, Her Highness Maji Chandravatiji Sahiba. She was a woman of piety and charity who worked for the welfare of the poor in Bikaner despite her *purdah*. When she died unexpectedly in 1909 Ganga Singh poured out his grief in a letter to the Prince of Wales (soon to be King George V) who had visited Bikaner a few years before. Ganga Singh's first wife had died in 1906 and as his second had proved unable to have children, he married for a third time in 1908, in accordance with the Hindu religion. By this marriage Ganga Singh had one surviving son, Prince Bijey Singh. Appropriately, perhaps, the Maharaja's first biographer KM Pannikar records neither the names of his second or third wives nor of his second daughter. For the record, the Maharaja's second wife was the daughter of Thakur Ganga Singh of Bikaner, his third the daughter of Thakur Bahadur Singh of Bikamkore and his surviving daughter was Princess Shiv Kanwar who was born in 1916. Also in accordance with the times, when the Maharaja celebrated his silver wedding anniversary in 1933 'he spoke of the Maharani [his third wife] in public for the first time'.[22]

Like other princes, the 21st Maharajah was an autocrat in a feudal age. There was something of a lawless frontier province about Bikaner with its notoriously unruly *thakurs* and weak administration. He laid down his authority right from the beginning. His first speech, as an 18-year-old, began: *The first thing that I want to say today is something about the past. A minority of eleven years is a long time and if the people have no strong hand over them they go wrong. I am sorry to say that intriguing parties have been the ruin of Bikaner ... I wish it to be known that I strongly disapprove of bribery. God help the men who give and take bribes because I certainly will not help them.*[23]

Early on in his reign, the Maharaja dismissed his *dewan* (prime minister). This was partly to personalise his government, and partly to stop it being undermined by the *dewan*, who was working under the orders of the officious and interfering Political Agent Captain Bayley. Bayley assumed a reforming and innovative ruler was a threat to British interests and close contact with the *dewan* was one way to control him. 'I do not agree with you [in your dismissal of the *dewan*]', he wrote to the Maharaja, 'the system worked well during the minority.'[24] But Bikaner had his way, at the cost of constant polite but argumentative letters exchanged between them over the years.

Here is not the place to recount how the Maharaja subdued the *thakurs* and modernised his state, to the extent of introducing over 70 Acts in the first thirty years of his reign. One example will serve for many: the management of the great famine that afflicted the state at the very beginning of the Maharaja's reign. Following several years of drought, only six inches of rain fell in 1898 and the summer of 1899 was completely dry again. The parched desert yielded no crops and livestock died in large numbers. Such was the misery the population began to migrate north into the Punjab and then, to add to this misery, cholera, smallpox and measles further decimated the population. The young ruler's first initiative was to send in his army, the Bikaner Camel Corps, as a kind of relief agency. This was predictable in a country where, now as then, the army is one of the institutions that works. His second initiative was inspired. Like US President Franklin Roosevelt in the Great Depression of the 1930s, Bikaner employed his people on public works. Borrowing money from the leading *seths* (merchant class) and from outside the state, he undertook modernising projects that would eventually be remunerative. Nine irrigation projects, two railway lines, three roads, ten miscellaneous works including the extension of the city wall of Bikaner, were all carried out over this period. Relief centres staffed by doctors were opened. Interest-free loans were advanced to farmers against whom no cases of fraud or embezzlement were recorded. The Maharaja himself was everywhere, touring the villages on horseback with only three small tents for himself and his staff. He planned the massive undertaking; he attended to the detail. Particularly for an 18-year-old, this was an extraordinary achievement. As Curzon said, awarding him Queen Victoria's *Kaiser-i-Hind* gold medal: 'His Highness of Bikaner was his own famine officer, throughout the fearful time, and he conducted his campaign with indefatigable energy and skill.'[25]

Ganga Singh's own conclusion was that a famine should never occur again if human enterprise and skill could prevent it. He decided there and then on a vastly ambitious scheme to provide water. This was the Gang Canal, eventually opened in 1927, which carried water from the Sutlej River in the Punjab to convert 1,000 square miles of the desert scrub of Bikaner into green and pleasant fields. It took the Maharaja 28 years and twenty separate schemes to raise the money and obtain the permissions. After that 500 new villages sprang up in only ten years, and the vast loans were not only repaid but the state earned a steady revenue. One of the reasons for the Maharaja's effectiveness was simply his patience.

In 1902 the Maharaja of Bikaner visited Great Britain for the coronation of Edward VII. He was a great success. The King-Emperor declared he had a strong regard for his 'opinion and counsel' and obviously for his majestic bearing too, for he was invited to stand behind His Majesty at state functions and appointed ADC to the Prince of Wales. The Maharaja had found his future role in Europe: a majestic ornament on state occasions and a giver of sensible advice. It is notable in how many group photographs of the high and mighty he is standing behind the central seated figure, sometimes the King-Emperor himself, often the Viceroy or Prime Minister. In part this was because he looked like the Western ideal of a Maharaja and excelled in living up to that image. In part it was because he spoke perfect English and held views royalty and statesmen liked to hear – un-intellectual, undoubtedly loyal, but understanding the mood of the times. He also liked a good gossip and boasted about his ability to tell anecdotes in a cockney accent. After he visited England again in 1910 to attend the Coronation of George V, a royal Private Secretary wrote to him rather patronisingly: 'His Majesty is much struck by your command of the English language, and your letter, written without a mistake in spelling or phraseology, reaches a high standard of English scholarship.'[26]

Incidentally, although Ganga Singh was bilingual in English and Hindi, he spoke the local Marwari language when at home. A traditionalist, he insisted on 'the dialect of our fore-fathers'. He would put down visitors who spoke Hindi with the phrase *Deshi gadhi poorvi chal* ('Local donkey with a foreign swagger').[27]

As far as British royalty was concerned Bikaner had another attraction: he loved shooting game and arranging efficient hunting parties. He was a man after King George V's own heart. When the Prince of Wales, as he was then, visited India in 1905, he called in at Bikaner for a few days of shooting. On this occasion the game was sand grouse and on Gajner Lake the royal party of 11 guns bagged 2,841 birds in two days. Then they had a go at wild pigs. The hunt diary recorded: 'Four boars were speared by the Prince and his staff, one of which showed stubborn fight and gave the English visitors an excellent idea of what a Rajputana pig could be.'[28] Going on a *shikar* (hunt) was mandatory whether the British guest was a sportsman or not, and sometimes the returning Viceroy would swap experiences with King George V. Lord Irwin said he had shot so many grouse 'he was glad he took the King's advice and padded the butts of his guns with India rubber'. Poor Lord Reading confessed to King George V he was a shooting duffer 'who had only wielded a golf club or a legal affidavit'.[29] He had fired 1,700 cartridges but only added 336 birds to a bag of 6,988 (!).

Between 1898 and 1914 a constant stream of British VVIPs

(Very, Very Important Persons, to use Indian terminology) called in to visit the Maharaja – the Viceroy Lord Curzon in 1902, the Duke of Connaught (brother of King Edward VII) in 1903, the Prince of Wales in 1905, the Viceroy Lord Minto in 1906 and 1908, and Lord Hardinge in 1912 and 1913. That same year, 1913, the future Secretary of State for India, Edwin Montagu, paid a visit and wrote in his diary his views of his future Peace Conference colleague: 'The more I saw of Bikaner, the more I liked him. The swagger which I did not notice in England, and the rather over-emphasised affection of English slang, vanish before one's realisation of his great business ability, his devotion to the interests of the state, and his great popularity among the English and Indians who serve under him.' [30]

On top of this entertaining, the Maharaja was a member of the committee that laid on the Coronation *durbar* for King George V when he visited India in 1911, the first time a reigning British monarch had done so. It had an inauspicious beginning. The Indian princes advised that the King-Emperor should enter Delhi on an elephant, for centuries the symbol of imperial rule. Instead King George chose a horse, and as he was not that good a horseman, he rejected the Viceroy's coal-black thoroughbred standing 17 hands high, and chose instead a small, docile horse of no striking appearance. Wearing a white *topi* (sun helmet) that covered much of his face, the King-Emperor was scarcely recognisable, and those that did spot him were disappointed.

The *durbar* made up for it. *The Times* (of London) of 13 December described perhaps the most splendid occasion in the history of India in suitably grandiose language: 'Enthroned on high beneath a golden dome, looking out to the far north from whence they came, their Majesties the King-Emperor and the Queen-Empress were acclaimed by over 100,000 of their subjects. The ceremony at its culminating point exactly typified the oriental conception of the ultimate repository of imperial power. The Monarchs sat alone, remote but beneficent, raised far above the multitude, but visible to all, clad in rich vestments, flanked by radiant emblems of authority, guarded by a glittering array of troops, the cynosure of the proudest princes of India, the central figures in what was surely the most majestic assemblage ever seen in the east.'

As the historian David Cannadine wrote, 'The image of India protected and projected by the Raj – glittering and ceremonial – reached what has been called its "elaborative zenith" at the Coronation durbar of 1911.' Yet as King George's biographer Kenneth Rose commented, and Cannadine repeated, 'the British Raj depended less on justice and good administration than on precedence, honours and minute distinctions of dress'.[31] No wonder the Maharaja of Bikaner was so conscious of his status. *The Times of India* referred to him in an article the following day: 'Standing by the side of the King-Emperor, the soldierly figure of the Maharaja of Bikaner attracted much attention. The Coronation *Durbar* brought him prominently to the public eye and made his personality familiar to the leaders of British India.'

THE BRITISH RAJ
'Raj' is simply a Hindi word meaning 'rule' as also in maharaja. It was the name given by the British to their rule in India, but only after they left in 1947. Before then the words used were 'Empire' or 'British Empire'

By 1914 the city of Bikaner had been transformed from a medieval frontier capital with its Junagarh fort, choking bazaars and crumbling *havelis* (grand courtyard mansions) into the makings of a modern town with imposing public buildings given imperial names like the Hardinge Municipal

Hall or the Irwin Municipal Assembly, wide highways and public parks. The centrepiece of the modern town is the Lallgarh Palace commissioned by the Maharaja during his Regency. Designed by an English architect in the Indo-Saracenic style, but built and decorated by local craftsmen, its 'out and out grandeur' (to quote the *Lonely Planet* guide) must have impressed any VVIP. The Palace is pink sandstone, with marble courtyards and formal gardens where peacocks strut among the bougainvillaea. Within, hanging balconies, lattice carvings and wall mirrors add to the splendour.

The Maharaja set up a representative Assembly for his people in 1912, on the Silver Jubilee of his accession to the throne. One of his strengths was his understanding of the spirit of the times, although he was rooted in the traditions of his princely state. Bikaner had been a feudal state with a military tradition and a limited education system, so at first the representative Assembly was little more than a 'talking shop'. It had the right to discuss all proposed legislation but not to enact it, and it also had a limited franchise. Nevertheless, it was a start. As the Maharaja said: *All that I aim at, at present, is to initiate a system under which my subjects will be trained to become efficient members of a really representative Assembly when the time comes.*[32]

Now the Maharaja considered that his time had come to move onto the national stage politically. Until Lord Hardinge became Viceroy in 1910, the princely states were regarded as isolated units, forming no relationship with each other or as a body with the Government of India. This was intentional. Any political or even social contact between princes was looked on with disfavour in Calcutta. This had been so since the time of the East India Company, because it feared any combination between 'Country Powers' might lead to a challenge to its military power. Incredible to relate, even the Maharaja of Bikaner, who was used to entertaining royalty, had to obtain the permission of his Political Agent before he paid a social visit to a princely neighbour. At *durbars* and other princely gatherings a strict watch was kept, and reports were made to the Government about which princes were seeing a lot of each other. This isolation was not altogether one-sided. Some of the princes of India, jealous of their status and sovereignty *vis-à-vis* each other, regarded any kind of political gathering as a threat. And the Nawab of Hyderabad or the Maharaja of the Kashmir, whose kingdoms were the size of much of Europe and nearly as wealthy, had little in common with, say, the tiny princely state of Junagadh in Gujarat.

Such isolation could not continue into the 20th century. Even the absolute imperialist Lord Curzon wanted the princes to be 'factors in the administration', as we have seen, and in 1904 he formed a Chiefs' College Conference. Here the attending princes humbly passed the Viceroy a collective note in which they said: 'What we, one and all, do feel most strongly about is that we are ready and willing not only to offer our advice but to spend our time and labour on important matters which involve wide public interests.'[33] But nothing came of it.

Bikaner, however, was made of stronger stuff. He saw Hardinge was sympathetic to a more co-operative relationship and he feared that unless the princes, who after all owned one-third of the land of India, could speak with one voice, then the changes imminent in the governance of British India would leave them on the sidelines. The relocation of India's capital from Calcutta to Delhi in 1911 encouraged his thinking, for it brought the government closer to the heart of India. In 1914 he composed a careful note for Hardinge

THE MAHARAJA OF BIKANER

that became a seminal document: *The present juncture is one of a very serious crisis for the* [princely] *states and they feel most gravely the danger of being left behind and shut out altogether. They do not wish to become mere puppets and to share the fate of some European aristocracies. They feel they are complementary to the democratic element in India. They represent the people of their states and speak for them at the gate.* With remarkable prescience, the Maharaja foresaw a new constitutional structure for the whole of India: *A federal chamber representing all the princely states together with the provinces of British India as well – would gradually grow up with, at first, advisory functions.*[34]

> **They [the Indian princes] do not wish to become mere puppets and to share the fate of some European aristocracies. They feel they are complementary to the democratic element in India. They represent the people of their states and speak for them at the gate.**
>
> **THE MAHARAJA OF BIKANER, 1914**

Hardinge was enthusiastic. He summoned a Chiefs' College Conference to Delhi where, on 3 March 1914, the Maharaja converted his note into a speech. *The Times of India* gave its backing: 'The seed capsule of the Maharaja of Bikaner's speech was an urgent appeal for closer organic connection between the [princely] States and the Government of India. It has an unanswerable force. India before our eyes is developing rapidly and the Native States cannot stand and gaze.'

Then the First World War broke out and any constitutional change was put on hold, but the Maharaja had given himself his life's work from then on. Moreover, he was now a leading soldier and statesman on the national stage with royal connections in Britain. He was the clear choice to represent the Indian princes internationally. His performance in London during the Imperial War Cabinet and Conference of 1917 and then in Paris during the Peace Conference of 1919, was to further develop his conviction that the princes should play an important part in India's movement towards autonomy.

2

The Indian Army in the First World War

In September 1900, the young Maharaja became the first Indian prince to go overseas to fight under the British flag. He and his Camel Corps (dismounted), known as the *Ganga Risala*, were part of an Indian Expeditionary Force that sailed to China to quell the Boxer Uprising, so-called because some of its leaders were members of a secret society that used a clenched fist as a signal of recognition. This was an anti-foreigner, anti-imperialist revolt of considerable ferocity that resulted in the deaths of tens of thousands of Chinese Christians and hundreds of Europeans. In January 1900 the Chinese Imperial Court issued an edict defending the rebellion, and so contingents of the Imperial Army joined it. In June Chinese troops besieged the foreign legations in Peking (now Beijing) close to the Forbidden City. It took a so-called 'Eight-Nation International Alliance Army' of over 50,000 (mostly Japanese, Russian and British) to fight its way through to Beijing and relieve the foreign compounds. By late September, when the Maharaja arrived at the head of his *Ganga Risala*, the worst of the uprising was over and only mopping-up operations remained. This was his first experience of warfare and he acquitted himself well, being 'mentioned in despatches'. The voluntary and courageous service of the Maharaja appealed to Lord Curzon, who was keen to involve the forces of the princely states in the defence of the Empire. When Bikaner returned to Calcutta in December 1900 he was greeted with acclamation and awarded the China Medal. However, a far sterner and more challenging war lay ahead.

On 4 August 1914, the British Empire declared war on Germany. The Maharaja saw this as a glorious opportunity to emulate his ancestors, the Bika Rathores, 17 out of 21 of whom had led their own troops in battle. He instantly sent a cable to the King-Emperor couched in terms of medieval chivalry: *I have the great honour and privilege of having served Your Imperial Majesty as Aide-de-Camp longer than any other Indian Chief. I implore Your Imperial Majesty most earnestly, if the Empire is involved, to give me an opportunity for that personal military service which is the highest ambition of a Rathore Rajput Chief. I should esteem it the highest possible honour ... I am ready to go anywhere in any capacity for the privilege of serving my Emperor ... This is the opportunity of a life-time ...*[1] Bikaner was not the only prince to see himself in this light. *The Times of India* used a similar phraseology in August 1914: 'The swords of the martial Princes leapt from their scabbards.' Little did they know what was to come.

In fact, surprising as it may seem from today's perspective, the Indian sub-continent was never so united as it was in August 1914. Even Mohandas Gandhi, in London when the war broke out, rallied his countrymen by pledging them to offer 'all humble assistance as we may be considered capable of performing as an earnest of our desire to share the responsibilities of Empire'.[2] Most probably his real motive, shared by the educated classes in India even if they were not politically active, was to show that in taking her share of the Imperial burden, India was worthy of self-government.

The Indian allegiance had its share of *realpolitik* too, for the future of the British Empire was at stake. If Britain remained neutral then Russia threatened to renew its confrontation in Persia and Central Asia, a further chapter in the so-called Great Game to capture India's North-West Frontier. If Germany and Austria-Hungary proved victorious, the British navy would be beaten and the colonies defeated. When the Ottoman Empire joined the Central Powers on 31 October 1914, the World War came to India's doorstep, for her near neighbour, Mesopotamia (present-day Iraq), was now hostile. Moreover, German imperialists could exploit their alliance with the Turks to move men and materials down through the Balkans and Turkey to Aleppo, Baghdad and Basra and then up into Afghanistan and Baluchistan, thereby provoking the unstable North-West Frontier with India. This, in fact, is exactly what the Germans were to do in 1916. The base line was clear: few Indians wanted to exchange British domination for German.

However, most of the 683,000 Indian soldiers under arms at the War's end (another 300,000 were non-combatants[3] in supply and transport services) did not fight to bring self-government to India, or to keep India in the British Empire. Nor were they fighting for the King-Emperor, although he was a revered figurehead. They fought for the honour of their regiments, and this was the distinctive character of the British Indian Army.

Traditionally, in the Old Indian Army as it was called later, battalions were formed on a 'class company' basis, meaning a racial and religious basis. A typical battalion from the Punjab, for example, would consist of two companies of Punjabi Mussulmans (Muslims), a company of Sikhs and another of Jats. This made proper observance of religious and caste distinctions easier, neatly expressed at this time by the famous iron ration, the Sheikhupura Biscuit. This was identical for all rankers but came in different wrappers: those for Hindus certified Brahmins manufactured them under priestly supervision, and those for Muslims certified Islamic mullahs approved them. The lesson of the infamous Enfield cartridge (allegedly greased with pig and cow fat) that supposedly caused the Mutiny of 1857 had been learned well.

This 'class company' gave a regiment its solidarity. What added to it, indeed made the British Indian Army regiment unique, was its family character. Men in every company were drawn from specific areas, as were the Viceroy's Commissioned Officers (VCOs) or junior officers of the regiment. They knew each other and in many cases belonged to the same family. Their senior British officers identified with them too, speaking the soldiers' language and often taking leave in their villages. The platoon was the focus of the soldiers' loyalty, then ultimately the regiment, but not the British Indian government. This was drummed into the VCOs of the Indian Army, the vital links between officers and men. As described by K Subrahmanyam, Director of the Indian Institute of Defence Studies, in 1989: 'The British conditioned him [the VCO] to be totally apolitical. He was not in the Army to fight for either the country or the King Emperor. He had chosen the army as a career as generations of his forefathers did. He had sworn an oath of loyalty on his religious book and participated in the traditional salt taking ceremony and his duty was to uphold the honour and glory of his platoon, then his company, then his battalion and then his regiment. While credit must be given to the British for having correctly evaluated the Indian (mainly Hindu) ethos and having raised the British Indian army according to it, the ethos itself goes back to millennia-old concepts of Hindu society. The bearing of arms was a profession and loyalty to the oath undertaken and the honour and glory of the unit were all that mattered, so long as there was an assurance that the social values and framework would not be changed.'[4]

Regimental spirit could be seen at its best in the Old Indian Army. It was essentially a warrior tribal affair, sometimes even an affair of villages. A young soldier knew if he did not do well in battle he had to face the scorn of his village. The traditions of the regiment were taught at the *mandir* (Hindu temple), *masjid* (mosque), *guruwara* (Sikh temple) and church parades, and of course on mess nights when new recruits were expected to recognise each trophy and piece of silver. The family ethos of some regiments was so strong that an officer about to marry had to ask permission of his commanding officer in the presence of his 'brother' officers. This regimental spirit is still alive today nearly a century later. In fact some fighting families have five generations of service in the same Indian regiment.

In 1914, when the Indian soldiers arrived in France, they received a message from the King-Emperor that reinforced this tradition of regimental pride and religious obligation: 'You are the descendants of men who have been great rulers and great warriors. You will recall the glories of your race. You will have the honour of showing in Europe that the sons of India have lost none of their ancient martial instincts. In battle you will remember that your religions enjoin on you that to give your life doing your duty is your highest reward.

History will record the doings of India's sons and your children will proudly tell of the deeds of their fathers.'[5] And when they died the regimental histories recorded that they died not for 'King and Country', as is inscribed on memorials in every British village, but 'in the assurance that their sacrifice was not in vain and the example they set inspired their successors to win fresh laurels for the regiment'. Another regimental history recorded: 'They have given their lives nobly to perpetuate the name of the regiment and to prove beyond all question the fighting quality of the Marathas.'[6]

Frederick Sleigh Roberts, Field Marshal Lord Roberts of Kandahar (1832–1914) was born at Cawnpore in India and became one of the most revered military heroes of the Victorian age. The relief of Kandahar in the Second Afghan War of 1878–80 by his Kabul Field Force after a legendary forced march secured his fame. He was Commander-in-Chief, India from 1885 to 1893, and was made Field Marshal in 1895. Following the early defeats in the Second Boer War, Roberts was sent out to take command in South Africa in 1900. He later campaigned for conscription, and died of pneumonia at the age of 82 while visiting British troops on the Western Front.

In fact, most of the fighting regiments of the Old Indian Army came from the north of India. This was due in no small measure to the racial prejudices of Field Marshal Lord Roberts VC whose seminal views moulded the British Indian Army not only in 1914, when he died, but up to the eve of the Second World War. He had fought in the Indian Mutiny of 1857 and ended his career in India in 1893 as Commander-in-Chief; *Forty One Years in India* was the title of his autobiography. In other words, he was a 19th-century soldier whose prejudices moulded a 20th-century army.

His first prejudice was a racial distinction between 'the martial races' of India and the others. 'No comparison', he wrote, 'can be made between the warlike races of northern

India and the effeminate peoples of the south.'[7] He instigated a policy of 'Punjabisation' so that in 1914 half the infantry battalions in the British Indian Army were drawn from the Sikhs, Jats, Dogras, Hindus and Muslims of the Punjab, a further quarter from the Pathans and Baluchis of the North West Frontier Province and others from the martial races of Nepal, primarily the Gurkhas. The successors to the old Madras Army who had stood firm under Clive at the Battle of Plassey and marched north to defend the East India Company during the Mutiny a hundred years later were no longer valued, nor were what Roberts called dismissively the 'so-called fighting Marathas of Bombay'. As for the old Bengal Army that had mutinied in 1857, it had been disbanded and its soldiers found themselves bottom of the list. British officials in Calcutta regarded Bengalis as *challaki*, or 'too clever by half' and this prejudice was confirmed in a revealing report of 1930 that stated 'broadly speaking one may say that those races that furnish the best *sepoys* [native infantrymen] are emphatically not those which exhibit the greatest accomplishments of mind in examination.'[8]

The second prejudice of Lord Roberts was that Indian soldiers, however brave, did not make good officers. Being an officer himself he did not mince his words: 'It is the consciousness of the inherent superiority of the European that has won for us India. However well educated and clever a native may be, and however brave he may have proved himself, I believe that no rank that we may bestow upon him would cause him to be considered an equal by a British officer. Native officers can never take the place of British officers. Eastern races, however brave and accustomed to war, do not possess the qualities that go to make good leaders of men.'[9]

In 1914 every officer in the British Indian Army was British, from subaltern to commander-in-chief. It was only the loss of British officers on the Western Front that forced a policy of 'Indianisation'. The lack of Indian officers commanding Indian troops was an affront to Indian nationalists. Not long after the war Motilal Nehru (father of Jawaharlal Nehru, the first Prime Minister of independent India) spoke out with vehemence: 'I may say at once that the word Indianisation is a word that I hate from the bottom of my heart. What do you mean by Indianising the Army? The Army is ours and we have to officer our own Army. What we want is to get rid of the Europeans of the Indian army.'[10] When SP Sinha became President of the Indian National Congress in 1915 he argued forcibly that every Indian male should have the right to enlist in the British Indian Army, irrespective of race or province of origin and that the officer ranks should be thrown open to all classes of His Majesty's subjects.

The Maharaja of Bikaner arrived in northern France in October with an appointment on the Headquarters Staff of the 7th Indian Division stationed near Bethune; from there he moved to the Headquarters Staff of the Commander-in-Chief of the British Expeditionary Force, Field Marshal Sir John French. The Maharaja saw no action, however, and was intensely frustrated. His Highness was not allowed to risk his life, for in Europe that heroic time when a prince was allowed to lead his troops into battle had gone. In January 1915 he needed to return to India because his daughter, Princess Chand Kanwar, was seriously ill; so on the way he visited his *Ganga Risala* in Egypt where it was defending the Suez Canal against a Turkish army.

The *Ganga Risala* was the only Camel Corps east of the Suez Canal, and it had been engaged in many patrols and skirmishes under British officers before its real commander arrived. In February 1915, the Turkish Army under Djemal Pasha attacked the Canal itself and, as luck would have it, a large contingent found its way blocked at Katib el Khel by the Camel Corps led by the Maharaja himself. A fight ensued and subsequently the Turkish Army withdrew, pursued by camels. This was the only action in which the Maharaja took part, and he did not return to the First World War. The *Ganga Risala*, however, covered itself in glory. It was in Egypt throughout the war, eventually numbering in the field 1,067 troopers, 166 'followers' and 1,254 camels. After its first engagement in the Sinai in November 1914 it fought many battles through to the end of the war and won many honours.

The first two Indian divisions reached the Western Front at the end of September 1914, and became engaged in a desperate defence near Ypres and Neuve Chapelle to prevent the German army reaching the sea. One third of the British sector of the Allied line was held by Indian troops, demonstrating what a vital contribution they made. Their baptism into the European War was hell on earth. Their experience in the dry, biting cold of the mountains of the North-West Frontier had been the sniper's bullet, the ambush on a lonely path, the charge of fanatical tribesmen. Their experience in the muddy, sometimes water-logged, trenches of Flanders was the high-explosive shell, the incessant machine-guns and mortars, and sometimes the poison gas preceding a German advance across 'no man's land'. Particularly grievous was the effect of severe losses on the family composition of the regiment. Most battalions had twelve British officers when they arrived at Marseilles; a year later no officers had survived in some battalions, and in others only one or two.

Yet the Indian soldier fought as his reputation required. A German soldier wrote for the *Frankfurter Zeitung* newspaper:

'Today for the first time we had to fight against the Indians and the devil knows those brown rascals are not to be under-rated. With a fearful shouting, thousands of these brown forms rushed upon us. At a hundred metres we opened a destructive fire that mowed down hundreds but in spite of that the others advanced. In no time they were in our trenches. With butt ends, bayonets, swords and daggers we fought each other and we had hard, bitter, work.' [11]

Indian fatalities on the Western Front amounted to 7,000 in 1915 alone. Moreover, the Indian soldier fought under even more psychological strain than the British Tommy. He was neither defending his home nor had he any chance of leave. He could not share a language outside his regiment. As the war went on, so a mood of resignation spread, but not defeatism. Many wounded Indian soldiers were nursed in Brighton hospitals, some in the Royal Pavilion itself, apparently because it was thought they might feel more at home in its 'oriental' surroundings, and a fuss was worked up in the press about white nurses tending brown men. The censor's report of their letters home notes the constant use of the word 'duty' and the unquestioned acceptance of the need to fight for 'King Emperor'. At the same time, their letters show a growing awareness of being Indian – 'Greetings to all Indians with you' – and a new view of the world. For those who returned home life would not be the same, and this impacted on growing Indian nationalism after 1918.

The Ottoman Empire was closer to home, and here, on the Mesopotamian front, the Indian Army controlled Allied operations. The Ottoman Empire consisted of Turkey, essentially the landmass of Anatolia, with a small extension west into the Balkans and then south-east to the Arab lands reaching to Persia. To attack Turkey there were four routes. The first was a direct thrust at Constantinople from the sea via the Dardanelles and Gallipoli. This was attempted in 1915, with disastrous consequences, although the 29th Indian Infantry Brigade was the only Allied formation to reach the summit of the ridge and look down on the waters of the Dardanelles. In all, 1,700 Indian troops were killed at Gallipoli. The second route was a land attack from Egypt up into Palestine, moving north and taking Jerusalem, then Damascus and then Aleppo by the Turkish border. On this front for the first year the Allied troops, including the *Ganga Risala*, were on the defensive, protecting the Suez Canal. Then, in 1917, General Allenby's army took the offensive. It invaded Palestine, captured Jerusalem and moved on to Damascus, at which stage the majority of Allenby's soldiers were Indian. The third route was from Russia down over the Caucasus Mountains, an entrance into the Ottoman Empire out of reach of any Allied army after Russia signed an armistice with Germany in 1917. The fourth route necessitated a march through Mesopotamia from the port of Basra on the Persian Gulf to the ancient Islamic city of Baghdad, then in Ottoman hands. This was a desert march of 400 miles, though supplies, such as they were, could be transported up the River Tigris. It was a route that appealed to the British from the beginning of the war, particularly as the fighting could be left to the British Indian Army because that area of Empire came under the India Office.

Over 600,000 Indian soldiers fought in the Mesopotamian Campaign led by British generals answerable initially to the India Office. One historian has labelled the generals 'a register of the infirm, myopic and bewildered' and the four-year campaign became known as the 'Mess pot'.[12] It was India's major contribution to the war, and a tragedy that British donkeys led Indian lions, to paraphrase a saying then current on the Western Front implying brave soldiers ('lions') were incompetently led by their senior officers (the 'donkeys').

The campaign began promisingly enough with a pre-emptive strike that captured Basra on 22 November 1914. Even then, confusion reigned, because the army commander was ordered to do nothing that would offend Turkish or Arab opinion, as if an unprovoked attack were not offence enough. Lord Hardinge was worried about what he called the 'Muham madan masses'; the 60 million Indian, mostly Sunni, Muslims who might well be sensitive to what was ultimately an attack on their spiritual leader. For the Caliph, the spiritual successor of the Prophet Muhammad as leader of the Sunni Islamic world was one and the same person as the Ottoman Sultan, Mehmed V. In fact, the Sultan had already called a *jihad* in defence of Islam though it had been, in the parlance of trench warfare, 'a dud'. Few Muslims had responded to it. Such was the anxiety about the loyalty of Indian Muslims, there was talk in the British Cabinet of setting up a rival 'caliphate' in Mecca as the centre of a British-sponsored Muslim state in Arabia and Mesopotamia. The future of the 'caliphate' was to become a major issue for India at the Paris Peace Conference. However, during the Mesopotamian Campaign, the sensitivity of Indian Muslims never became the serious issue the India Office feared.

The advance alongside the Tigris gained momentum. In September 1915, General Sir Charles Townshend's 6th Indian Division captured Kut, less than 30 miles from the magnet of Baghdad. He advanced a further eight miles to Ctesiphon where on 22 November his British and Indian troops were unexpectedly and disastrously defeated by a well-prepared Turkish force. Over 4,000 were killed or wounded, many by marauding Arabs who finished off and robbed those left on the battlefield. Townshend retreated back to Kut, a small Arab town lying in flat and featureless land in a narrow loop of the Tigris, some of it below the level of the river. Here his army was besieged for 147 days.

It now became apparent that the Mesopotamian Campaign was disastrously under-resourced. Compared to a Turkish army of 80,000 supplied from nearby Baghdad, the British Indian Army of 25,000 was 380 miles from its base. It soon ran out of food. In fact, in Kut rations were reduced to four ounces of grain per man per day with nine ounces of horsemeat. Eating this indigestible meal was virtually impossible because of the clusters of sand flies that 'bit hard'. The water was unsterilised because prevailing wisdom believed that flies, not water, carried cholera and dysentery. Beer ran out and so did ice. There were virtually no means of communication whether telephones or signals. The medical supplies were woeful, with not a single nurse in place until April 1916. That summer native craft converted into crude hospital ships sailed down the Tigris to Basra with their sides stained by dysentery and the sick onboard delirious. A lieutenant surveyed the torment and said to his sergeant, 'I suppose this is as near to hell as we are likely to see?' Drawing himself up as if he was on the parade ground, the sergeant replied, 'I should say it is, sir.' [13]

The Turks defeated an attempt to relieve Kut at the Battle of Hanna. After that the overall British Commander, General Sir Percy Lake, ignominiously and to the amazement of his superiors in London, offered a £2 million ransom to the Turks for the safety of the defenders of Kut. It was rejected with contempt. And so, on 29 April 1916, General Townshend surrendered. His surviving army of 12,000 men was forced on a veritable death march to Baghdad, starved, desperate for water, diseased and harried by Arabs all the way. At Ctesiphon, a British officer on a boat watched the prisoners 'dying with a green ooze issuing from their lips, their mouths fixed open, in and out of which flies buzzed'.[14] Over 4,000 died or were killed along that 30-mile route. In the whole campaign, 29,000 Indian troops lost their lives.

The Mesopotamian Campaign was a terrible disaster so far. It was compared to the First Afghan War of 1841, when the aged and dithering General William Elphinstone led his army on a winter retreat from Kabul down the Khyber Pass to Jellalabad, with all but one man dying on the way. An official enquiry confirmed the errors in administration and moved the command from the India Office to the War Office. General Sir Stanley Maude was put in command, and everything which the earlier campaign had failed for the lack of now began to arrive. Defeats became victories. Kut was retaken in February 1917 and Baghdad captured on 11 March. When this happened the British explorer and expert on Mesopotamia, Gertrude Bell, opined: 'That is the end of the German dream of domination in the Near East. Their place is not going to be in the sun.'[15] The drive further north up the Tigris ended at Tekrit where Maude died of cholera in November 1917. Then it was decided in London to transfer troops from the Mesopotamian front to Palestine where General Sir Edmund Allenby was about to begin his final push to Damascus. He captured it on 1 October 1918, thereby ending many centuries of Ottoman rule. The Ottoman Empire itself surrendered on 30 October.

An important intermediary between the British and Ottoman governments was General Townsend, who had been living in some luxury on an island near Constantinople as a prisoner of war after surrendering at Kut with the loss of 10,000 men. In mid-October he had been released by his captors and sent by motor boat to a Greek island from where he dispatched the Ottoman peace terms. These led to the longest British Cabinet meeting of the war.

Mesopotamia remained under the charge of the India Office, and some there wanted to keep it as a province of India with an open invitation to Indian settlers. At the Foreign Office, on the other hand, Arabophiles wished Mesopotamia to become a client state ruled by Prince Feisal, the son of the Emir of Mecca. This alarmed the India Office, who saw the danger of encouraging independence for the Arabs while discouraging it for Indians. The future of Iraq, as it became, was a matter for the peacemakers. We experience the result of their deliberations today.

The Indian Army had stayed true to its salt (the ceremony of eating salt in the regimental mess was a sign of loyalty). The sum of its sacrifice was 79,000 men killed in action. A roll call of the dead is inscribed on a massive memorial arch designed by Sir Edwin Lutyens and raised in the Raj capital of Delhi. The sacrifice of so many Indians who fought in a World War, the causes and character of which they could scarcely understand, was not lost on the peacemakers shortly to assemble in Paris.

3

SP Sinha and the Indian National Congress

Soon after David Lloyd George became Prime Minister at the end of 1916, he decided to summon an Imperial Conference. Mindful of the challenge of the Canadian Prime Minister some years before – 'If you want our aid, call us to your councils'[1] – Lloyd George was well aware that this aid amounted to over two million soldiers, over half of whom came from India. Imperial Conferences had been held before the First World War, but none since it had begun, and senior representatives from India had never been invited. Lloyd George changed that. He also decided on two different forms of meetings, held on alternate days: a Conference when matters of long-term interest would be discussed, and an Imperial War Cabinet where British Ministers would meet with the Prime Ministers of the Dominions and their Indian counterparts to deal with matters of the war on a day to day basis. 'I regard the council as marking a new epoch in the history of the Empire',[2] Lloyd George told a journalist.

When the Maharaja of Bikaner and Sir SP Sinha met in London for the Imperial War Cabinet and Conference in

March 1917 they came together from very different backgrounds. Bikaner, soldier and socialite, was the Maharaja of a desert kingdom in west India. Sinha was a lawyer and intellectual from cosmopolitan Calcutta in the east, until recently the capital of British India. Their appearance showed they came from different worlds. While Bikaner was almost a caricature of the fighting Maharaja, Sinha looked every inch the small, dapper lawyer – short black hair not covered by a turban, penetrating eyes in a serious, intelligent face, a white collar and bow tie above his barristers' tabs and a black jacket below. While the Maharaja sported a luxuriant moustache, the lawyer's was neatly clipped. What they shared, however, was the ability to feel equally at home in England and India, and a political aspiration to work for Indian autonomy within the British Empire. They were nothing if not loyal to the British Crown.

Little is known in India about Satyendra Prassana Sinha, although, measured in terms of British achievement, his *curriculum vitae* was impressive. That is the point, for in his public life Sinha became more an adopted son of the British Raj than an Indian citizen. He was born in 1863 in Raipur village in the Birbhum district of West Bengal to the north of Calcutta. Here his father was a *zemindar*, a tax-collecting landlord, and a senior local government official. Sinha won a scholarship to the Presidency College in Calcutta, married when he was only 17 and then left for England, without a degree and without his wife, in secret. This secrecy may seem irresponsible and out of character, but less so in India, because it was due to the firm Hindu beliefs of his father who would have deplored the idea of him leaving the land of his birth and travelling overseas. So the young Sinha arrived in England without money; but undeterred, he won a scholarship to Lincoln's Inn to continue his legal studies. One may only imagine the determination and self-confidence this must have taken.

He later said he met leading British politicians and legal tutors in London who treated young Indians on equal terms with their British counterparts, provided only that they met in the same spirit of intellectual enquiry – a marked difference to the prevailing racism in much of London society. From these years or soon after must date the start of his friendships with, for example, William Wedderburn, who was one of the founders of the Indian National Congress (INC) in 1885, and James Bryce, the historian and professor of civil law; both of them Liberal MPs. Had he stayed longer he would also have encountered the young Muhammad Ali Jinnah, the future founder of Pakistan, at Lincoln's Inn. As it happened, he got to know Jinnah well in the Indian Congress a few years later. It was a seminal time for Sinha. Before he returned to India in 1886, having qualified at the Bar, he had already made the connections and acquired the intellectual grounding on which his later career was founded.

It was at this point Sinha and his wife Gobinda, who was about to bear the first of his seven children, became converts to the Hindu sect of Brahmo Samaj. Even in India, that most religious of countries, the community of Brahmo Samaj is not only very small (numbering today perhaps 20,000) but also very elite. It represents a form of enlightened Hinduism that, for example, decries both the caste system and the subjugation of women, is opposed to scripture as authority and to any kind of priesthood. Its adherents 'embrace truth, knowledge, reason and freewill'.[3] It seems an ideal philosophy for a left-wing lawyer about to lead his people towards self-rule, and so it was to prove. The sect's most famous adherent was Rabindranath Tagore, the Bengali poet, philosopher and Nobel Prize winner who studied law in England at about the same time as Sinha. Unsurprisingly they were friends.

Sinha became a lecturer in law at City College, Calcutta, and built up a successful practice at the Bar. He was an outstanding lawyer and advocate: quick, lucid and penetrating in argument; painstaking and clear-headed in research. He specialised in constitutional law, and in 1903 he was preferred to a British barrister for the appointment of Standing Counsel to the Government of India. Two years later he was also appointed Advocate-General of Bengal. Thus he became the constitutional legal adviser of the governments of both India and Bengal at a most sensitive time, for it was in 1905 that Curzon attempted to partition Bengal. This was to prove the most controversial and disastrous of all his policies. For a Bengali to advise between headstrong imperialists and outraged Bengali resisters, who saw partition as the virtual vivisection of their homeland, required supreme tact; and Sinha displayed it.

Curzon regarded Bengal as simply too large a province to govern efficiently, so he decided to cut it in two. The eastern regions (much of present-day Bangladesh) were joined with Assam in a new province, while the western regions based on Calcutta were joined with Bihar and Orissa. Splitting the province in this manner meant Muslims were in the majority in the east and Hindus in the west, a division that was to have dire consequences. Touchy Bengalis saw this as a blatant imperialistic policy of divide and rule imposed with the usual British arrogance and disregard for public opinion. Nationalists throughout India took up the anti-partition cause particularly in Calcutta where riots, petitions and boycotts of British goods were everyday occurrences. A Bengali novelist, Bankimchandra Chatterjee, composed an anthem 'Bande Mataram' ('Hail to the Motherland') and eventually this became, in 1947, the national anthem of India: 'Mother sweet, I bow to thee; Mother great and free!'

The partition of Bengal became a serious threat, both to British rule and to the stability of India, for two reasons. The first was that Calcutta had always been the centre of political dissent, much of it revolutionary in an intellectual sense, and what happened in Calcutta today could spread through India tomorrow. The second was that the defence of Bengal became synonymous with a homeland for Hindus, so Muslims, who hitherto had opposed partition, began to look on the new province in east Bengal as their own homeland, free from the domination of Calcutta. The seeds of a later partition were sown in 1905. The two halves of Bengal were re-united in 1911, but the damage had been done.

We know Sinha regarded the partition of Bengal a mistake that would 'leave behind a legacy of bitterness', but what private turmoil he must have suffered we do not know. His personality remains elusive. It must have been considerable, because on the one hand he was a legal adviser to Curzon's government, and on the other he was now a member of the Indian National Congress, the formal opposition to British rule. Whatever his feelings, they did not impede his career.

In 1909 Lord Minto, Curzon's successor, appointed Sinha a legal member of the Viceroy's Executive Council, so he became the first Indian to be a member of the British government of India and to share its collective responsibility. He was an unpopular choice among the British establishment, both at Cabinet level and in the Viceroy's own Council. Apparently even King Edward VII voiced his objections. Anglo-Indians in Calcutta, who regarded themselves as superior to Indians, were said to be consumed with 'fury and wrath'.[4] Racism was much more blatant then than now and Sinha was certainly subjected to racial abuse, but not so intensively as later when he joined Lloyd George's government and was given a peerage.

Lord Minto was a liberal who took seriously the Royal Charter of 1858, promulgated by Queen Victoria after the Mutiny, that 'neither race nor creed should be a bar to employment in public service'. Defending his appointment of Sinha he said he had 'no intention of taking a narrow interpretation of a promise which was as wise and politic as it was just'.[5] It is worth quoting Queen Victoria's advice, given in 1899, and endorsed by her grandson, King George V: 'The future Viceroy must really shake himself more and more free from his red-tapist, narrow-minded, council and entourage. He must be more independent, must hear for himself what the feelings of the natives really are, and do what he thinks right and not be guided by the snobbish and vulgar, overbearing and offensive behaviour of our civil and political agents. We must not trample on the Indian people and continually remind them they are a conquered race.'[6]

When Sinha resigned from the Viceroy's Council in 1910 to rejoin his practice because he could not afford to neglect his work at the Calcutta Bar, Lord Minto wrote to King Edward to say what a success he had been. Five years later, in 1915, Sinha was elected President of the Indian National Congress at its annual meeting in Bombay.

The INC was, some said in India, His Majesty's Loyal Opposition or, as an early Congressman called it, 'the germ of a Native Parliament'.[7] It had been founded in 1885 on the advice of a British civil servant, Allan Octavian Hume, as a platform for civic and political dialogue between educated

Indians and the British government. 'Educated' meant an English-style education, and in its early days Congress was demonstrably loyal to the Queen-Empress. She was called 'Mother' and her name cheered by the assembled Congressmen at every annual meeting. Congress meant nothing to the ordinary people of India and it did not concern itself with them, or with their poverty, ignorance and ill health. Nevertheless, in the patronising voice of the times, it did claim to be the voice of India: 'The English-educated Indians represented the brains and conscience of the country, and were the legitimate spokesmen of the illiterate masses – the natural custodians of their interests, and those who think must govern them.'[8]

The political objective of the INC was to hold Britain to its promise that the British government in India existed for the benefit of Indians who, under its guidance, would advance to a state in which they could manage their own affairs. This had been the accepted vision statement since 1858 and was, of course, both vague and highly debatable. Today the accepted view is that the British Raj existed primarily for the benefit of the Raj. However, when Sinha became President in 1915, the aim of the INC was, as ever, to hold the British to their promise of eventual self-management for India within the benevolent British Empire. 'We are British subjects', declared its father-figure, Dadabhai Naoroji, 'and if the British failed to treat Indians as such then the British would be no better than Asian despots.'[9] The function of Congress was twofold: to lobby Calcutta and London, and to serve as a forum for educated Indian opinion regardless of religion or geography.

This self-satisfied and obedient approach characterised the INC for its first 20 years, but it could not last. The partition of Bengal incensed educated Indians and awoke religious animosities. In 1906 Congress split between the moderates like Sinha and extremists led by Bal Tilak, the first Indian to embrace *swaraj*, or complete self-rule, as the only solution. He urged the abandonment of all things British and the adoption of direct action, based on the violent riots and boycotts taking place at that time on the streets of Calcutta. Tilak's Hindu nationalism further alarmed the Muslims of India such that some of their leaders left Congress and founded the All India Muslim League in 1907.

Tilak's arrest and imprisonment quietened things down, although it is worth noting that the Viceroy Lord Hardinge was injured in an assassination attempt in 1911. The abandonment of Bengal partition helped too. Then India entered the war in 1914 and, as we have seen, the consensus inside and outside the INC was that loyal participation would show India was deserving of self-government. But consensus never lasts long in a volatile and disparate country like India, particularly when it is at war; and in 1916 an extraordinary German-Turkish plot was uncovered that could have caused a nationwide revolt.

Although most Indian Muslims stayed loyal to the Empire despite its attack on the Ottoman Caliphate, a German mission to Afghanistan promising arms and money managed to stir up the so-called 'Hindustani fanatics', precursors of the Taliban in the wild tribal areas of the North-West Frontier. A quisling ruler called Kunwar Pratap, in fact a minor and deposed Maharaja, was installed in Kabul as head of a

BAL TILAK (1856–1920)
A militant nationalist, he believed the end of *swaraj* (complete self-rule) justified any means. Unlike his successor Gandhi he preached violent revolution and was imprisoned twice for doing so at the turn of the century. True to his own dictum that 'the Extremists of today will become Moderate tomorrow', he supported India joining the war in 1914, became President of the Home Rule League and talked with Montagu about reform in 1918. He was called 'The Father of Indian Unrest'.

'Provisional Government of India' and he formed a vague 'Army of God' to take on British rule in the name of Islam. Even more bizarre was a simultaneous German plot to stir up a mass insurrection in Bengal armed with weapons smuggled through Siam (Thailand), so the Raj would be threatened from east and west. The uprising in Calcutta was timed for Christmas Day 1915. This over-ambitious plot was suppressed by British intelligence, and a Defence of the Realm Act enabled the British government in India to intern terrorists and traitors without trial by jury. Nevertheless, it was a sign that deep in the interior of India a vast people could be stirred to challenge British rule. One result of the First World War and its aftermath was to bring these forces to the surface.

Just as bizarre as the German-Turkish plot of 1915 was the presence in India of Mrs Annie Besant, who formed the Home Rule League in 1916. The former wife of an English clergyman, then a militant atheist and advocate of free love, she had arrived in India in 1893, aged 46, and soon become head of the Theosophical Society in Madras. This was a religious movement that combined the reactionary with the modern. It venerated ancient Hindu traditions that predated Western civilisation and believed in modern social reforms. Her combination of the spiritual with the political appealed to educated Indians, who regarded her book *Wake Up India!* (1913) as a call to action for a peaceful *swaraj*. Annie Besant had Congress eating out of her hand, and in 1918 she would be elected its President.

This, then, was the state of Indian nationalism when Satyendra Sinha was elected President of the INC in 1915. His opening speech was that of a lawyer, but a lawyer with a clear political vision: 'Political wiseacres tell us that history does not record any precedent in which a foreign nation has with its own hands freed from bondage a people which it itself has conquered. But India was never conquered in the literal sense of the word and is not legally a possession of Britain. No other nation than Britain has fought so continuously and strenuously for freedom and the liberty of other nations. There is only one goal and only one path. East and West have not met in vain.'

He spoke for the mood of the majority when he went on to say that the autonomy of India within the Empire should be the accepted goal of Congress. Indians should become 'fellow-citizens of a common Empire'. As for the means of achieving this, he was quite clear. There were two ways: '1) Force. This is an abhorrent idea, unrighteous and criminal. I call on Indians to express in unmistakable language their abhorrence of dastardly crimes which besmirch the fair name of the country. *Swaraj* does not mean that Independence may only be achieved by the murder of Europeans. 2) By patience and wisdom; endeavour to advance by gradual, wary, steps.' [10]

> 'No other nation than Britain has fought so continuously and strenuously for freedom and the liberty of other nations. There is only one goal and only one path. East and West have not met in vain.'
> SP SINHA

So far Sinha's speech was unexceptional. Indeed, its sentiments had probably been expressed every year at Congress. But then he threw down a challenge to the British rulers: 'The British nation must declare their ungrudging approval of the goal to which we aspire, to declare their inflexible resolution to equip India for her journey to that goal.' [11] In other words, Sinha demanded the end of vagueness about self-rule. How serious were the British about it? What exactly did the British mean by it? What would the next steps be?

The Maharaja of Bikaner was asking much the same questions. When the two envoys to the Imperial War Cabinet and Conference met in London in 1917 they were determined to get answers. The stage was set for the next act in the long history of Britain's relations with India, and the peace negotiations in Paris leading to the Treaty of Versailles were to play a part in this.

4

The Imperial War Cabinet and Conference, March–May 1917

The British Prime Minister, David Lloyd George, was a Liberal Imperialist who believed the Empire could only be held together on the basis of national freedoms. In 1901 he declared: 'We ought to give freedom everywhere – freedom in Canada, freedom in the Antipodes, freedom in Africa, in Ireland, in Wales, and in India. We will never govern India as it ought to be governed until we have given it freedom.'[1] This was, of course, a paradox and in the end he could not resolve it, any more than could loyal Indian statesmen like Bikaner or Sinha. But with India he made a sincere start in 1917.

Although India had been specifically excluded from the Imperial War Cabinet and Conference in 1907 on the grounds that it was not a self-governing country like the so-called White Dominions, and this exclusion had pertained ever since, Lloyd George had no time for this distinction. India should be invited in view of its outstanding contribution to the war. Nor had he any difficulty in accepting the advice of Lord Chelmsford that the representatives should be the Maharaja of Bikaner and Sir SP Sinha. They represented the old elites, however reforming they were, and not the new nationalism that was beginning to take over Indian political life. Their loyalty could be relied upon. Lloyd George reacted to Bikaner with his usual open-hearted enthusiasm: '"Bikaner" as he was familiarly and affectionately called – the Indian Prince – was a

'We will never govern India as it ought to be governed until we have given it freedom.'
LLOYD GEORGE, 1901

magnificent specimen of the manhood of his great country. We soon found that he was one of "the wise men that came from the East". More and more did we come to rely on his advice, especially on all questions that affected India.'[2]

The Maharaja did, indeed, look magnificent, particularly when wearing the uniform of his Camel Corps with a great turban and glittering decorations. Aged 37, he was in his prime; over six feet tall with a broad chest, greying hair, piercing eyes and a luxuriant moustache, his complexion darkened by long exposure to the Bikaner sun. No wonder he was lionised by London society.

Yet the word 'representatives' needs to be read with care. The actual status of Bikaner and Sinha in the Imperial War Cabinet was as 'Assessors', advising the Secretary of State for India, Austen Chamberlain, until he was succeeded by Edwin Montagu in July 1917. The Imperial War Cabinet needs defining too. It sat in parallel with the British War Cabinet with British Ministers responsible for the management of the present war, but its constitution was different. In fact the title 'Cabinet' was novel. It had no Prime Minister, Lloyd George presiding as *primus inter pares* (first among equals). Its members had neither collective responsibility nor executive authority. Even majority decisions were impossible as no Dominion could be required to sacrifice its freedom of action.

Nevertheless, the Imperial War Cabinet was the best available forum in which leaders of the Empire could share in the formulation of Imperial policy about war and peace. The Canadian Prime Minister, Sir Robert Borden, called it the Cabinet of Governments. Lloyd George was proud of it, writing in his *Memoirs of the Peace Conference*: 'The meetings of the Imperial War Cabinet were no formal and perfunctory make-believe *Sanhedrins* [the old Hebrew assemblies or "sittings together"] of the elders and chief priests of the Empire, to give an appearance of consultation. There were genuine discussions of all questions of policy.'[3]

The Maharaja of Bikaner would relish the unique chance the Imperial Conference gave him for advancing the princes' political agenda as much as the status that would be conferred on him as a member of the Imperial War Cabinet. In anticipation of his new role, he gave a keynote speech in Bombay on 17 February 1917, on the eve of his departure from India. The occasion was a banquet held in his honour by his fellow princes. He said he spoke *for the first time publicly not only as a ruler of a great state, but as an Indian statesman.* Then he went further, calling in effect for greater reforms in the administration of the whole of India, both the princely states and British India: *I sincerely believe that British statesmanship and sense of justice will accord to our country that place to which her position in the Empire entitles her.*[4] This was vague, certainly, but the British could not argue any longer that the demand for reforms in India were confined to Bengali *babus* (intellectuals) and young firebrands shouting for Home Rule. Now it came from the pro-British Indian aristocracy. The speech made an impact, not least among his fellow princes. As his first biographer, KM Panikkar, wrote: 'Political India gasped in surprise, but friend and foe alike realised that this open declaration in favour of reforms by a representative of the Ruling Princes selected by His Majesty's Government as a spokesman at the Imperial War Cabinet and Conference, to a gathering of Princes, had changed the complexion of the Indian political movement.'[5]

The Maharaja and his entourage arrived in London at the end of February 1917 and stayed at the Ritz Hotel. His 'majestic' bearing (to quote Lloyd George again) combined with his new official status meant he was lionised by London society. Sir SP Sinha lodged much more modestly with his friend Sir William Wedderburn in Hampstead. There is no evidence that either the Maharaja or Sinha suffered from any form of racial prejudice on this occasion, though it would be mistaken to think even majestic Maharajas were exempt from it. In 1919 Lady Diana Cooper sat next to the Aga Khan at the Ritz and even this innocent act affronted the Lord Great Chamberlain: 'The sight of natives entertaining smart society women is not pleasant,'[6] he whispered. King George V, however, who regarded himself as the 'father' of 400 million Indians, was strongly opposed to this sort of mindless colour bar. At a royal lunch he made this clear by placing the Maharaja of Bikaner on the Queen's right (this was during his 1919 visit) in preference to British grandees. In fact King George himself pointed out that although Bikaner and Sinha had been made honorary members of the best clubs in London, they still would not be admitted to British clubs in India. At about this time, the Prince of Bihar asked the writer Somerset Maugham: 'Do you know the difference between the Yacht Club in Bombay and the Bengal Club in Calcutta? In one they don't allow either dogs or Indians, in the other they don't mind dogs.'[7] So King George gladly gave patronage to the Willingdon Club in Bombay, which was one of the few with mixed-race membership. As a further example of the small-minded bigotry of the British class system, a court decided Indians like Sinha who received honorary knighthoods were not entitled to use the prefix 'Sir'. Again, King George put a stop to this.

At the same time, the King-Emperor liked his Indians to look like Indians. He ticked off Bikaner, who prided himself in his British language and manners, for appearing at the Imperial War Cabinet in 'a bowler hat and a suit of *dittos* [a morning suit], rather than *puggaree* [an Indian turban]'.[8] This must have mortified the Maharaja.

The Maharaja of Bikaner received the Freedom of the City of London and a Doctorate of Laws from the University of Edinburgh. In just one week he made four formal speeches: at a lunch held by the Lord Mayor of Manchester (23 April), at another held by Indian delegates of the Empire Parliamentary Association in the House of Commons (24 April), at the Guildhall in London and at Mansion House the same day (1 May). These speeches expressed, in the somewhat overblown language of the times, his complete loyalty to the King-Emperor: *The Crown is the indispensable keystone of Empire. It does not fetter our perfect freedom; it is not only the supreme symbol of the unity of the Empire but the surest pledge of democracy for a great part of the globe* (Manchester, 23 April). *My brother Princes charged me to lay at the feet of His Imperial Majesty the King-Emperor an earnest assurance that India's Princes will spare no effort to co-operate in the cause of Empire* (The Guildhall, 1 May).[9]

Simultaneously, he constantly pressed the British government for greater Indian self-rule. Significantly, at the Empire Parliamentary Association lunch on 24 April in the presence of Ministers and MPs he said: *Our aspiration is to see our country attaining, under the standard of our King-Emperor, that self-government and autonomy which you in this country secured long ago and which our more fortunate sister Dominions have enjoyed for some time past. I am prepared to admit it presents a difficult problem. But is it insoluble by British statesmanship and goodwill?*[10]

Referring to the princely states that enjoyed *a unique status in the British Empire having come under the suzerainty of the King-Emperor* he pointed out that over 10 per cent of them now had *representative institutions*, and this number was growing. The next obvious advance would be to set up a Council of Princes where important matters concerning the British government could be discussed, similar to the Legislative Assemblies in British India. He ended by pointing out the *legitimate unrest* in India was surely connected with the slow rate of change.

The Imperial War Cabinet met for 14 sessions between 20 March and 2 May. Bikaner and Sinha witnessed discussion of some of the most momentous events of the First World War – the Russian Revolution, the entry of the United States into the war, the climax of the war at sea and the desperate but doomed attempts by Lloyd George to dissuade his generals from launching the offensive of 'Third Ypres' in July. The Indian Assessors made the most of their attendance at the Imperial Conference too. At its end, Sinha summarised their achievements as twofold. The Conference had formally rescinded the 1907 resolution that India should not be represented at its meetings and replaced it by a resolution that in future it should. Moreover, Lloyd George himself had declared that in future Conferences the Secretary of State for India should sit as a member of the British Cabinet and that India should be fully represented by its own members.

To critics in India who complained this was not enough, that these members would in reality be representing the British government of India, Sinha replied with asperity: 'True, each of the Dominions possesses responsible governments, whereas India does not at present, but would these critics prefer that India should not take its place in the Conference until she came completely self-governing, and did they expect that after eight weeks stay in England we would bring back in our pockets an ordinance making India a completely self-governing country at one bound? As far as I know, no-one has even asked for such a catastrophic change.'[11]

As is normally the case, off-duty socialising at the Conference was probably more useful than what happened in the chamber. Sir Robert Borden, the Canadian Prime Minister, certainly thought so: 'I invited members of the Conference to meet informally at the hotel at which I was staying and we had a full, free and frank discussion of the whole situation as far as the Dominions are concerned. I found it of great advantage that we had representatives of India there. Sir Satyendra Sinha stated the case from the India standpoint with great ability and fairness, and very deep feeling. The net result was the conclusion at which we arrived [on India being treated like a Dominion].'[12]

The real achievement of Bikaner and Sinha was to show the British establishment that advocating the cause of Indian freedom, with reservations, was not sedition but legitimate agitation. And India's share in the tragedy of war had increased both its right to be heard and the affection it attracted from the British public. Now the Secretary of State for India, Austen Chamberlain, asked His Highness the Maharaja of Bikaner to send him his detailed views on Indian reform. This he did just before he returned to India in May. He polished up his paper on the train to Rome and had it couriered back, with a note: *My dear Mr Chamberlain, I regret I could not hand it over to you before leaving England but the rush was very great. I apologise for its length and the poor paper and ink, but it has not been an easy matter dictating it and having it typed during this trying journey. Yours sincerely, Ganga Singh.* The Maharaja embarked for Bombay on 15 May.

The 'Rome Note', as it became known, was indeed a frank paper. Gone were the prolix, fulsome phrases more suitable for a post-lunch oration. The Maharaja was specific. He put forward a four-point programme:

1. *The vital necessity of a formal and authoritative official declaration by the British Government that its ultimate objective and goal in India is self-government within the British Empire.* Later in the same paper he added, frankly: *If the granting of self-government within the Empire is not the goal, then it is impossible to conceive what the goal is.*
2. *The advisability of inaugurating further political reforms in the Legislative Councils.*
3. *The desirability of greater autonomy being granted to the Government of India as well as to Provincial Governments.*
4. *The vital importance to the Indian States of establishing a Council of Princes to deal with matters which concern the British Government on the one side and the States on the other.*[13]

Unfortunately for Austen Chamberlain, he had to resign from the Government almost immediately after receiving the Rome Note as a result of the debacle in Mesopotamia. He was replaced as Secretary of State for India by Edwin Montagu. The historic and controversial Montagu-Chelmsford Declaration of July 1918 that proposed reforms in the government of India partly stemmed from the Rome Note written by the Maharaja of Bikaner. But before we see what happened to it, we must introduce the third member of the triumvirate that represented India at the Peace Conference in Paris; the 'Jewish Briton' (as he called himself) who loved India, Edwin Montagu.

5
The Montagu-Chelmsford Reforms

Edwin Montagu had fallen in love with India during his first long visit in 1912–13 as Under Secretary of State for India, and for much of his short political career he aspired to become Viceroy. He wrote his first unsolicited letter of application to Prime Minister Herbert Asquith in 1915: 'I want to see a Viceroy who will try to be an energetic administrator rather than a mock royalty surrounded by out of date and rather tawdry pomp – one who goes to India attracted by India rather than by the dignity of the office, one who will improve the system of representative government, consider without prejudice the demands born of India's share in the War, organise the independent states and decentralise the Government. These are the problems which above all others in the world I want to tackle. I am quite prepared to abandon all hope of ever being asked to do anything else.' Then he addressed himself to possible objections: 'There is the question of my race. That is the serious obstacle. It is an objection which you must balance against other considerations. It is an objection of civil servants and perhaps soldiers. As regards the Indians I do not believe it to be an objection. I have not canvassed for opinions, but I have received spontaneous and oft-repeated entreaties to go to India from: The Aga Khan – a Mohammaden; Bikaner – a modern and highly esteemed Rajput ...'

Montagu wrote letters that were frank to the point of indiscretion, and this was no exception. He continued: 'You can only choose a Viceroy from one of three categories:

a) Men whom you want to get rid of, e.g. Kitchener [Secretary of State for War]
b) Men you want to reward, e.g. Lord Derby [War Secretary]
c) Men chosen for their knowledge and desire to deal with Indian affairs. I claim to belong to this category.'

He concluded: 'I can conceive nothing which would cause me more sorrow than the abandonment of this ambition.'[1]

The 'objections' to which Montagu referred were simply because he was a Jew in an age in which anti-Semitism was commonplace. This mattered more when appointments to the India Office were made because many of the old India hands, known as 'Die-Hards' who would rather 'die' than give up British India, were frankly racist. Before Lloyd George appointed Montagu as Secretary of State for India in 1917 he consulted the Foreign Secretary, Arthur Balfour, who responded: 'Montagu is very able; he knows a great deal about India; he would be very popular with the Indians. I'm certain he would be disliked by the Anglo-Indians [the British in India] because he is too much of a reformer and partly because he is a Jew.'[2] In the words of Lloyd George's pre-eminent biographer, John Grigg, 'Montagu conformed all too well to the Jewish stereotype that existed in most gentile minds. By turns self-assertive and self-abasing [the letter above is a good example], he inspired feelings of aversion and distrust that were compounded by ethnic prejudice.'[3]

Poor Montagu! He was doomed to sorrow for he never did become Viceroy, despite writing a similar letter of application to Lloyd George during the next vacancy in 1920. Nevertheless, he was probably more highly regarded by Indians than any other British statesman of this era. He was right when he said, 'I am an Oriental. In India social relationships which English people find so difficult come quite easy to me.'[4] For example, when he and Lord Chelmsford (the successful candidate) visited India in 1918, Chelmsford refused to be garlanded with flowers while Montagu embraced this charming Indian welcome with enthusiasm. Montagu found Chelmsford the stereotypical Briton, 'cold, aloof and reserved.' He himself was a warm-hearted champion of Indian reform. When he died prematurely in 1924, aged 45, a booklet was published in his honour in India: 'How steadfastly and whole-heartedly Mr Montagu championed the cause of the Musalmans [sic] in India so long as he was Secretary of State. What a pity [we] did not recognise, support and help him as a friend as we should have done'.[5]

Montagu was in fact as much a friend of Hindus as Muslims, but it is easy to see how some contemporaries considered he held a bias towards Islam. In 1917 he actually opposed the Balfour Declaration promising Jews a homeland in Palestine. His main contribution to the Peace Conference as Secretary of State for India would be to oppose plans dividing Turkey and to accuse the Allies at the Conference of 'taking sides against Islam'. In fact he resigned over this issue in 1922. No wonder the Indian encomium quoted above began: 'Edwin Montagu was perhaps the most enigmatic personality of his time. He seemed to embody in his own person all the great-ness and mystery of his race.'

Born in 1879 into a banking family, Montagu entered Par-liament in 1906 as a passionate Liberal. Ten years later he was in the Cabinet, the third Jew ever to be so (after Benjamin Disraeli and Herbert Samuel), at the early age of 36. He was one of Asquith's protégés until in 1915 he married the young Venetia Stanley with whom the Prime Minister had an open *tendresse*, which made relations difficult. Venetia Stanley con-verted to Judaism to marry Edwin Montagu but it was not a happy marriage.

Montagu was a strong admirer of Lloyd George, and when Lloyd George became Prime Minister in 1916 after the *coup* that ousted Asquith, he followed him into the Coalition Govern-ment as Financial Secretary to the Treasury. Here he tried to mend relations between the pre-vious and present Prime Minis-ters, an attempt that ended with him being mistrusted by both parties. His appointment as Sec-retary of State for India was the right post for him at the right time. It soon enabled him to leave behind the personal stresses of life in London on a tour of India from where he wrote home that he dreamed of accomplishing 'something big and epoch making'.[6]

COALITION GOVERNMENT
In December 1916, Prime Minister 'wait and see' Herbert Asquith was forced to resign over his inert conduct of the Great War by fellow Liberal David Lloyd George, a far more dynamic wartime politician. Lloyd George became Prime Minister but he split the Liberal Party. Nearly all his Cabinet were Conservatives, including two former Prime Ministers, Andrew Bonar Law and Arthur Balfour. The Coalition Government lasted until October 1922. The Liberal Party never recovered.

Yet he was not a happy man. The semi-autobiographical *Edwin Montagu, A Memoir and an Account of his Visits to India* has a chapter headed 'I am Not Liking Life', and the frontispiece photograph of Montagu, taken towards the end of his life, shows a sad-looking intellectual with a large, bald, domed head, bright but sorrowful eyes and a lip slightly curled in defiance. When he died in 1924 his obituary in *The Times* pointed indirectly to his difficulty in relationships: 'In his lovable and complicated character great subtlety of intellect was curiously mingled with simplicity of mind. He had the trustfulness of a child; it was often betrayed, and he suffered agonies of disappointment and surprise, but his confidence always returned ready for the next encounter. He was often angry but never embittered.'

Perhaps this is why India appealed to him, for it is a country of extroverts where warm friendships are readily made. Montagu used the Parliamentary debate on the Mesopotamian Report in June 1917 as a virtual application for the post of Secretary of State for India, for he knew Austen Chamberlain was going to announce his resignation in the speech after his. He began by aiming at the India Office, an easy target: 'The Government of India is too wooden, too iron, too inelastic, too ante-diluvian, to be of any use for modern purposes. It produces an apotheosis of circumlocutory and red tape beyond the dreams of any ordinary citizen. Unless you are prepared to remodel this century-old and cumbrous machine, then, I believe, that you will lose your right to control the destinies of the Indian Empire.' He went on to describe the future that he desired: 'I see the great Self-Governing Provinces of India organised and coordinated with the great Principalities not as one great Home Rule Country, but a series of self governing Provinces and Principalities, federated by one Central Government.'[7] At the centre, he went on, British paramountcy was to remain for the indefinite future. This was enough to get Montagu the job, and he was appointed Secretary of State for India the following month.

It was a shrewd appointment, for not only was Montagu a lover of India, but his ideas of reform were cautiously pitched. Few in government doubted reform towards self-rule was necessary. A spirit of patriotic nationalism was stirring India. As we have seen, Indian soldiers were conscious they were fighting for 'the rights of nations, great and small' and fighting united them in patriotism for Mother India. Some of them picked up the mood of change. A Labour Corps trench-digger wrote home that the British government fully recognised the self-sacrifice of India and the new Labour Party and 'many other great sahibs'[8] believed in an Indian government. The recent Russian Revolution encouraged Indian radicals to believe that autocracy was not an impregnable fortress; it could be overcome and replaced by a popular government. Moreover, the Indian 'sacrifice,' as it was emotively called, was no longer only on the battlefields. Indian businessmen were well aware that from 1916 to 1918 a compulsory levy was charged for the war effort, and this increased by 10 to 15 per cent annually. Reformers were pushing against a half-open door because, facing the fourth year of the war, Lloyd George's government knew if it was to demand continuing sacrifices from India it had to make concessions towards self-rule. At the same time, Conservatives in the Cabinet, like the former Viceroy Lord Curzon and the Foreign Secretary Arthur Balfour, needed to be reassured any reform would not play into the hands of the All India Home Rule League, behind which the next generation

> 'The Government of India is too wooden, too iron, too inelastic, too antediluvian, to be of any use for modern purposes.'
>
> EDWIN MONTAGU, 1917

of less compromising Home-Rulers like Mahatma Gandhi, Jawaharlal Nehru and Muhammad Ali Jinnah were forming. So the Montagu-Chelmsford reforms, towards which the new Secretary of State worked for the next year, were a workable compromise. He had as his advisers the Maharaja of Bikaner and Sir SP Sinha, now regarded as the acceptable face of the Indian establishment in the west.

What was the professional relationship between the Viceroy and the Secretary of State for India? There was always tension between the Government of India in Calcutta or Delhi and the India Office in London, for the Viceroy's job was to govern while the Secretary of State's job was to represent the views of the British Cabinet, of which he was a member. Chelmsford was a statesman, not a politician, and he admitted he disliked Parliament, whereas Montagu said he found the administration in India bureaucratic and conservative. The reforms came from the genuinely liberal mind of Montagu whereas Chelmsford went along with them cautiously, knowing they represented the views of the British government. Reading the correspondence between them, it is clear Chelmsford, while sharing Montagu's reforming beliefs, felt he had his hands full attempting to keep the lid on a subcontinent simmering with unrest. Montagu, on the other hand, constantly worried that he was interfering. He wrote the Viceroy on 4 March 1919: 'I quite sympathise with your desire to reduce by one third or more the enquiries of the present Secretary of State. He is doubtless a most damnable nuisance.' And again, on 26 June: 'My own view is that the Secretary of State should go every year to spend a week with the head of every province and a week with the Viceroy. Great heavens above, if I were to suggest that policy!'[9] It was not an easy relationship.

On 20 July 1917 Montagu read out the objectives of the

forthcoming Montagu-Chelmsford proposals in the House of Commons. The so-called Declaration was immediately wired to India: 'The increasing association of Indians in every branch of the administration and the gradual development of self-governing institutions with a view to the progressive realisation of responsible government in India as part of the British Empire.'[10] As proof of the political minefield Montagu needed to negotiate, he had originally proposed to the British Cabinet the phrase 'the gradual development of free institutions in India with a view to ultimate self-government', but Curzon insisted this was dropped in favour of his own wording.[11]

In the summer of 1917, Montagu disappeared to India for a five-month tour to discuss what he regarded as his 'big and epoch-making plan'.[12] Amazingly, he was the first Secretary of State for India actually to visit the subcontinent. In anticipation of his arrival, the Maharaja of Bikaner organised a conference to discuss the whole question of relations between the princely states and the government of India. This resulted in a Note which Bikaner presented to Montagu in Delhi in December. Despite his efforts it showed his brother princes had many reservations. While they saw the need for a Chamber, they were suspicious of further encroachments on their independence and the removal of their privileges.

It has to be said a good deal of snobbery tarnished relations between the princes too. The Rajput chiefs looked down on the Maharatha princes and also on the chiefs of the Punjab who were Jat and Sikh. And so it went on throughout India. A few opposed the notion they would have to sit with 'commoners' in any legislative assembly. Behind the scenes, 'Die-Hard' British officials stirred up the resistance. For instance, Sir John Thompson, Chief Secretary in the Punjab, wrote in his diary against the name Montagu: 'a Knave'(!)[13]

In the end Montagu was able to reassure Chelmsford when they met later in the tour that there was enough consensus among the princes to devise a constitution for a Chamber, but that it would require tactful negotiation. In July 1918 the Montagu-Chelmsford reforms were published, although they only became law a year later. For this first step in the 'progressive realisation of responsible government in India', as the Declaration put it, Montagu and Chelmsford devised an ingenious constitutional device called 'dyarchy', literally government by two bodies independent of each other. The central government of India was to remain under the Viceroy's control and would be wholly British, although a Viceregal Legislative Assembly

> 'Liberty will not descend to a people; a people must raise themselves to liberty. It is a blessing which must be earned before it may be enjoyed.'
> INSCRIPTION ON BRITISH GOVERNMENT SECRETARIAT IN NEW DELHI

with Indian members would be set up, with mostly advisory powers. It was to be based in the new government buildings of New Delhi, then under construction. Visitors today may read the inscription on the Secretariat Building: 'Liberty will not descend to a people; a people must raise themselves to liberty. It is a blessing which must be earned before it may be enjoyed.' [14] (Today this sounds a patronising sentiment but it could have come from Montagu himself, for he said more than once that Indians were 'intellectually our children'.)

In the provinces, however, power was to be transferred to eight Provincial Assemblies in which Indian Ministers would take charge of education, health, agriculture and the state budget. This sounds a major step towards self-government, but the small print, as it were, was intended to impose shackles. The British were to keep control of taxation and security and they would be able to veto any legislation. They would also nominate one-fifth of the Assembly members. Indian representatives would be chosen by an all-male electorate amounting to five million, based on property ownership and rank in the Indian Army.

A Chamber of Princes was proposed too. Its function was to advise the Viceroy on questions affecting the princely states and matters concerning the states and British India jointly. The detail of its constitution was left open and joint working parties of rulers, *dewans* and officials of the British government were to meet in Delhi in January 1919 (when Bikaner was at the Paris Peace Conference) and again that September.

Montagu expected noisy opposition to the proposals. It came from the right. *The Spectator* said they were 'a kind of Bolshevism'. The *Saturday Review* lamented old authorities would be replaced by 'debating societies' and foresaw more trouble ahead if the proposals were adopted because Labour MPs, who advocated complete Home Rule for India, would be sitting on parliamentary committees overseeing Indian affairs. It was *The Spectator*'s language that really offended Sinha, over in Britain for a second Imperial War Cabinet and Conference held that summer. He abhorred racism and made his position clear in a speech: 'I take on myself to utter a grave warning against descriptions of "the masses of India" as "a vast block of uncivilised peoples" and "a pack of animals outside in the dark waiting to be fed". As sure as I am standing before you to-day these words will be translated into every vernacular in India and spread throughout the length and breadth of the land. The ill-mannered and ill-informed attacks will inevitably provoke reprisals which will hamper efforts for reform and will ferment prejudice against Britain.'[15]

Reaction in India among the emerging nationalist politicians was also critical. They foresaw that the Montagu-Chelmsford proposals promised much but would probably deliver little power into Indian hands. However, there was no guarantee in the summer of 1918 the proposals would ever become law.

In April 1918 Lloyd George decided to convene another Imperial War Cabinet and Conference. Once again, the Viceroy invited Bikaner – 'Your Highness has the advantage of entering the inner circle of the Empire's Councils with previous experience and knowledge,'[16] – but the Maharaja declined on the grounds of overwork so the Maharaja of Patiala went in his place. Bikaner missed an important five months in London (May–October) for on the Western Front the final German offensive was repulsed that summer. The Dominion Prime Ministers had gained in confidence since their first meeting a year before, and at the same time their confidence in the conduct of the war by the British generals had diminished. They demanded a direct voice in the plans of campaign, and Prime Minister Billy Hughes of Australia opined that had he been consulted he, for one, would have opposed the disaster of Third Ypres (Passchendaele). They also asked for an on-going relationship with the British Prime Minister in between these Imperial War Cabinets and Conferences, instead of 'having to meander through the channels of the Colonial Office' as Hughes put it.[17] Montagu said whatever was done for the Dominions should be done for India too. Discussion was shelved, and the war ended only a few weeks later.

> 'I ... utter a grave warning against descriptions of "the masses of India" as "a vast block of uncivilised peoples" and "a pack of animals outside in the dark waiting to be fed".'
> SP SINHA, 1918

At the Durbar of 1911. The King-Emperor George V and the Queen-Empress Mary are attended by senior Maharajas. The Maharaja of Bikaner stands at the right of the photograph

II
The Paris Peace Conference

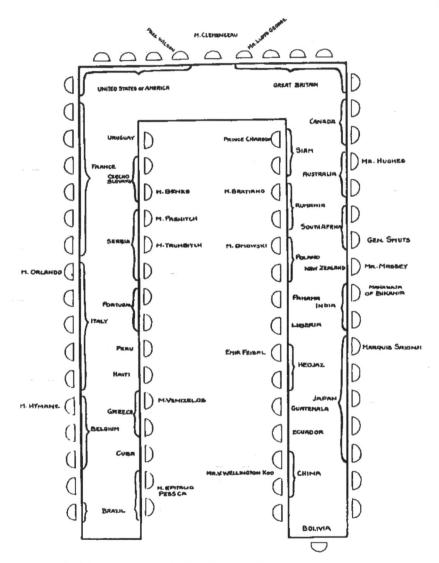

Sketch of the seating plan at the Paris Peace Conference.

6

The Call to Peace

The end of the First World War on 11 November 1918 took most people by surprise. They had thought the terrible suffering would go on forever. Only four days later telegrams were dispatched to Bikaner and Sinha summoning them to a third session of Imperial War Cabinet and Conference (as we have seen). They both booked passage from Bombay on the *Chindwara*, but because the ship was delayed, left instead aboard HMS *Dufferin*. They arrived in England in early December in the middle of the so-called 'khaki election', a vituperative campaign in which many of the electorate vented their hatred of Germany, pacifists and peacemakers, and the disagreeable life, including an epidemic of fatal influenza, to which the terrible war had reduced them. It was a period of political hiatus in which Bikaner and Sinha were left with little to do, although they had hurried over as commanded.

The Maharaja stayed as usual at the Ritz, firing off telegrams home to fill the time: *Send immediately all papers regarding Bikan assistance in the Mutiny* [this was the time when Maharaja Sardar Singhji had ridden to the rescue of the British and covered himself with glory]; *Send details of*

plague in Bikan [the influenza epidemic had hit India too];
Has new Doctor resumed duties as Palace Surgeon?; then a
tetchy note to the Comptroller of Bikaner: *Do stop waste* [*sic*]
money by putting 'England' after 'London' in telegrams.[1] He
was worried about the latest attempts in his absence to negotiate a Constitution for the Chamber of Princes. While still
aboard HMS *Dufferin* (2 December) he had wired a 'brother
Prince' *to inform you of the machinations of certain Political
Officers* [British] *in Central India who have been attempting,
with however good intentions, to stir up feelings of smaller
Princes. We are faced with a real danger to the unity of Princes
being broken. It has been insinuated that Your Highness and
Myself had formed a sort of clique, that we were voluble and
plausible but simply working for our own ends.*[2]

The General Election was held on 14 December, though
the results were not declared for another two weeks. In the
meantime the Imperial War Cabinet held several meetings to
discuss the vexatious matter of Dominion and Indian representation at the forthcoming Peace Conference (see below).
Another matter on the agenda was the imminent visit of
the President of the United States, Woodrow Wilson. Loyal
servant of the King-Emperor that he was, Bikaner spoke
out in Cabinet urging the President to delay his visit so King
George could spend a quiet Christmas at Sandringham. His
Majesty, however, agreed to delay his holiday and received the
President with all due pomp and ceremony at Victoria Station
on 27 December. Bikaner was there as ADC to King George,
standing just behind the monarch as usual. The Maharaja
watched the President alight from his carriage and without
bowing to the King and Queen merely shake their hands with
a perfunctory 'How-do-you-do'. The Maharaja was shocked
by this discourtesy, for in his mind a King-Emperor clearly

outranked an American President. He quietly withdrew into the background to avoid being introduced to Wilson. The King noticed and made the Maharaja greet the President. An international incident was averted.

A few days later, on 1 January 1919, a Royal proclamation summoned Bikaner to Paris: 'George, by the Grace of God, King of Great Britain, Ireland and of the British Dominions beyond the Seas, Defender of the Faith, Emperor of India &c, &c, &c, [summons] Our Most Trusty and Well-Beloved, His Highness Sir Ganga Singh Bahadur, Maharaja of Bikaner, Knight Grand Commander of Our Most Exalted Order of the Star of India, Knight Grand Commander of Our Most Eminent Order of the Indian Empire &c,&c, [to attend the Paris Peace Conference as a Plenipotentiary.]' He was given the royal backing for his work: 'Engaging and Promising, upon Our Royal Word, that whatever things shall be so transacted and concluded by Our said Commissioner, Procurator, and Plenipotentiary in respect of Our Empire of India shall, subject if necessary to Our Approval and Ratification, be agreed to, acknowledged and accepted by Us in the fullest manner, and that We will never suffer, either in whole or in part, any person whatsoever to infringe the same, or act contrary unto, as far as it lies in Our power.'³ It was these royal threads of verbiage and trinkets of honours that tied the aristocracy of the Empire so tightly to the Crown. No doubt Sinha received a similar Royal summons.

In the 1918 General Election, Edwin Montagu retained his seat as MP for Cambridgeshire and returned to the Cabinet as Secretary of State for India. He was one of the few so-called Coalition Liberals, apart from Lloyd George himself, to serve in a Cabinet that was nearly all Conservative. His immediate aim was to steer his Government of India Bill, based on the

Montagu-Chelmsford proposals, through Parliament, and to this end he wished to confer as much power as possible on his Indian adviser, Sir SP Sinha. He therefore decided to have him appointed Under Secretary of State for India with a seat in the House of Lords. This meant asking the King to award Sinha a peerage. George V saw the sense of this, as did Lloyd George, who could not care less about the honours system. This was not, however, the general feeling among the Establishment, to whom making an Indian a Lord was worse than calling a professional cricketer a Gentleman. The racism of the time clearly emerges from this letter written by Montagu to Lord Chelmsford on 10 January: 'I wonder what you will think of the appointment of Sinha? I had no time to consult you. It will be a fine thing for India and for our position in such countries as America to hear the Indian Government defended in Parliament by an Indian. It will be a fine thing for all those who indulge in racial obloquy to have to do it in the presence of an Indian, and it will give the best earnest of the reality of our intentions. I had a little doubt as to Sinha having the necessary courage but when I told him yesterday morning, instead of entreaties and imploring requests to ask his friends, he answered, after a few words of doubt as to his capacity, with a firm affirmative from which he has not receded. When I told him I had to give assurance that he had only one wife, he said with a smile that he had always found one wife enough.'[4] Chelmsford approved but could not resist quoting a Hilaire Belloc jingle that ends '... but he was black as tar'.

Montagu then told Lord Curzon, the former Viceroy and soon to be Foreign Secretary, who made pomp and circumstance his own prerogative. Montagu reported Curzon's reaction to Chelmsford in the same letter as that quoted above:

'I wish I could repeat to you the incident: Curzon: "Oh, but Sinha is not a Peer." Montagu: "Not yet" I said. "An hereditary Peerage for an Indian?" "Yes," I said. "Has the King assented? "Yes." "Does Sinha know?" "Yes." "Well then, it's no good saying anything?" "No." "I confess I don't want to say anything. I am so shocked, so surprised, so staggered I dare not trust myself to express an opinion. It may be a very good thing; I can at least see this, for it will increase your chances of getting your legislation through."'⁵

The London *Evening Standard* of 11 January was equally aghast at Sinha's appointment. It included Montagu in its racial references: 'What would be the reflections of Robert Clive and Warren Hastings could they but revisit Westminster and find a Jew and an Asiatic native of India in control of this great Dependency? This is a precedent which foreshadows the gradual association of the people of India with the rule of that country.'

Satyendra Sinha was now Lord Sinha of Raipur, nominally a Liberal but a member of the Coalition Government. And so, after these dramas of politics, protocol and, indeed, royal procedure, the three Indian Plenipotentiaries, as they were called grandly, left London for Paris in January 1919.

The British Empire delegation arrived in Paris in early January. Numbering over 400 officials, including advisers, typists and clerks, it booked in at five hotels near the Arc de

LORD CURZON (1859–1925)
George Nathaniel Curzon had more influence over British policy in India and the Middle East than anybody else during this period. He was a much-traveled Asiatic expert and statesman at the height of the British Empire. As Viceroy of India, 1899–1905, his vision was of the full trappings of imperial majesty but supported by a reforming agenda. As Foreign Secretary, 1919–24, he dismantled the Ottoman Empire with relish. Disliked by Lloyd George for his showmanship, it nevertheless led to his design for the armistice commemorations at the Cenotaph in 1919.

Triomphe. The Plenipotentiaries stayed at the Hotel Majestic and it was here the Maharaja arrived on 15 January. 'It was very like coming to school for the first time,' said one new arrival, 'hanging about in the hall and being looked at by those already arrived as new kids.'[6] Prime Minister Hughes of Australia described it thus: 'The "elect" all lived together in the Hotel Majestic, a magnificent caravanserai near the Arc de Triomphe, where the food was excellent and the company even better. Practically all the guests in the hotel were officials of embassies or members of one of the numerous committees. Consequently, human nature being what it is, the Hotel Majestic was a great sounding board, and rumours were as thick as leaves on Vallombrosa [a metaphor from a poem by John Milton].'[7]

Hughes probably had an unsophisticated standard of cuisine as he had started political life as a steward for the Sheep Shearers' Union. In fact the French cooks at the Majestic had all been replaced on grounds of security by British ones so the food was that of 'a respectable railway hotel: porridge, bacon and eggs in the morning, lots of meat and vegetables at lunch, and bad coffee all day'.[8] At least the Dominion and Indian delegates could charge their bar bills to the British government. Margaret MacMillan (incidentally a descendant of Lloyd George) gives an amusing description of the Empire delegates in her book *Peacemakers,* continuing the analogy of arriving at school: 'If the British were the masters and matrons, the Canadians were the senior prefects, a little bit serious perhaps but reliable, the South Africans were the new boys, good at games and much admired for their sporting instincts, the Australians were the cheeky ones, always ready to break bounds, the New Zealanders and Newfoundlanders the lower forms and then, of course the Indians, nice chaps in spite of the colour of their skin, but whose parents were threatening to pull them out and send them to a progressive school [Assuming the parents were the Indian National Congress and the progressive school was the movement for Home Rule, then there was not much evidence of it – yet.].'[9]

Lloyd George arrived on 11 January, together with Montagu, and stayed with his immediate entourage at a luxurious flat in the Rue Nitot. He wasted no time getting down to work. The very first meeting of the Peace Conference was on 12 January between the heads of the Great Powers: President Wilson of the United States, Prime Ministers Georges Clemenceau of France, Lloyd George of Great Britain and Vittorio Orlando of Italy. These, of course, were the Powers that had won the war, so when Clemenceau was asked to justify the mandate of the Great Powers he replied simply '12 million soldiers'. They decided, together with their Foreign Ministers and the addition of two representatives from Japan, that they would form a Council of Ten. This became known as the Supreme Council, an extension of the Supreme War Council the Allies had formed in the last year of the war. This met two or three times a day in the Quai d'Orsay, chaired by Clemenceau. However, as the only titular head of state, Wilson's chair was a few inches higher than the others!

No one was in any doubt where the power lay, and in March the Supreme Council shed Japan and the Foreign Ministers and reverted to being the Council of Four. That was reduced to the Council of Three the next month when Orlando went home in a huff. He had not concerned himself much with the formulation of the peace terms, except where Italy was concerned, and unlike the other three he could scarcely speak English. Wilson, Lloyd George and Clemenceau really were supreme. They alone decided on most of the Treaty of

Versailles. Their deliberations were secret and informal, as in the British Cabinet. Their decisions were delegated to various Commissions for ratification and wording, and presented to so-called 'Smaller Allies' at the point of signature, but they made the decisions. The Germans, of course, were not even invited until later, when they were shown the first draft of the Treaty of Versailles early in May.

If the Council of Four was like the Cabinet, then the national parliaments back home served as the constituencies. With the Plenipotentiaries attending the Peace Conference representing Powers Great and Small, the Commissions and Committees, the rows of technical experts, the visiting potentates and pressure groups (including the British suffragettes), there was assembled in Paris for that short, heady period a sort of world government. 'We are the league of the people,' said Clemenceau on the day before the ceremony of the Treaty signing, to which Wilson replied: 'We are the state.'[10]

What then was the status of the Peace Conference itself? The first question to be decided was which Powers should be represented. The answer was, only those Powers that had declared war on Germany, or broken off relations with it. The second question was what number of Plenipotentiaries was to be allowed to each Power. The answer was agreed at that first meeting of the Great Powers on 12 January resulting in a victory, as the British Empire delegation saw it, for the Dominions and India. The third question was what was the function of the Plenary Conference that the Plenipotentiaries were invited to attend. Its formal function was limited, for the Great Powers kept decision-making in their own hands and did not submit issues to the Conference until it had agreed them. In fact the Plenary Conference only met six times between 18 January and 28 June when the Peace Treaty was signed.

An exception, however, were the meaningful debates in the Plenary Conference and in Committee assembled by the Conference about the setting up of a League of Nations, an institution of particular importance to India. Informally, the Plenipotentiaries did matter, not least because they shared the same Secretariat with the Great Powers and, of course, it is the bureaucrats who are the custodians and conduits of information. Moreover, the Plenipotentiaries had the ears of the Supreme Council. At Lloyd George's discretion, of course, those of the British Empire delegation could enter the inner sanctum and present their arguments face to face when their interests were being decided.

It must have been an intimidating occasion. In the magnificent office of the French Foreign Secretary in the Quai d'Orsay, Chairman Clemenceau sat in his chair by a massive log fire, sometimes looking up at the ceiling with a bored expression. Wilson fidgeted a lot and got up to stretch his legs. Lloyd George was restless too, chatting when he was bored and passing comments. While the interpreter translated into French and back, assistants tiptoed about with maps and documents and waiters brought in refreshments. Intimidating or not, the inner sanctum of the Paris Peace Conference was, as we shall see, the scene of the Maharaja of Bikaner's first triumph.

The case of the Dominions and India for independent representation at the Peace Conference had come a long way over the previous year. At a meeting of the Supreme War Council in February 1918, it had been decided that at a future peace conference each of the five Great Powers would send five Plenipotentiaries. The British government had suggested giving one of its five to a Dominion or Indian delegate, and this had caused an uproar because it seemed a mere token gesture.

The colonial countries were popular in Britain as a result of their contribution to the war effort. The Prime Ministers of Canada and Australia particularly, Robert Borden and Billy Hughes, were no longer subservient to the British Cabinet and demanded to be heard. They were increasingly scornful of the way the war was being conducted. Borden referred to 'the incompetence and blundering stupidity of the whiskey and soda British H.Q. staff' and Hughes said later that in any future war the British government could certainly not take Australia's contribution for granted.[11] Over the ensuing months, notably in the third session of the Imperial War Cabinet meetings, they rammed home their point that this contribution should be measured in terms of bloodshed and loss of life, which made their sacrifices greater than that of the United States.

On 4 December the Canadian Cabinet had urged: 'In view of the war efforts of the Dominion, the other nations entitled to representation at the Conference should recognise the unique character of the British Commonwealth, as composed of free nations under one sovereign, and that provision should be made for the special representation of these nations at the Conference.'[12] As we have seen, Borden had threatened to go home unless this resolution was granted. Hughes had been equally insistent and probably ruder.

So, on 12 January, Lloyd George persuaded his fellow Great Power leaders to allow the Dominions and India one delegate each, like the minor states of Siam and Portugal. More uproar! 'It was all very inconvenient,' said one British diplomat, 'what was the Foreign Office to do?'[13] The answer, suggested by Borden, was to increase the representation to two Plenipotentiaries, like the smaller Allied nation of Belgium. This should apply to Canada, Australia, South Africa and

India (including the Native States) while New Zealand should be allowed one delegate (Newfoundland was considered too small to have separate representation). Lloyd George went back and raised the demand, expecting more resistance. He wrote afterwards: 'It seemed as if the French and Americans harboured a suspicion that this idea of Dominion independence and separate nationhood was an artifice of the wily Englishman to increase his representation at the Congress. Foreigners always suspect us of advancing the most altruistic principles for any scheme that promotes British interest.'[14]

Once again, the other Great Powers gave way, partly because of the argument that the number of delegates did not really matter as all voting in the Conference was to be unanimous. The more cynical view, taken by France, was that the quarrelsome Dominions would cause Britain a lot of embarrassment, and a longer view taken by the United States was that separate Dominion representation on international bodies like the League of Nations would lead to 'the eventual disintegration of the British Empire'. On 15 January, when the rules of the Peace Conference were announced, the British Dominions and India were classed as 'belligerent powers with special interests', empowered to attend Conference sessions when questions concerning them were discussed, with the number of Plenipotentiaries that they had demanded.

In theory, the Dominions and India had greater power, for they were also part of the British Empire delegation itself. This consisted in the main of British delegates, but its composition was to be decided depending on the subject under discussion. The Dominions had a say in this selection too, so in fact the Imperial War Cabinet was re-constituted on French soil. It might be wondered why India was included with the Dominions with so little argument. The truth was the decision among the Great Powers lay with Lloyd George, and he considered the matter closed after the Imperial Conference decisions of 1917.

From the beginning, Montagu, Bikaner and Sinha were the Plenipotentiaries, although Bikaner was named as 'Adviser'. Montagu referred to this in a letter he wrote to Lord Chelmsford on 22 January: 'One of the adlati ['advisers'] becomes in theory and in practice a member [Plenipotentiary] and the other in practice but not in theory also a member.' In the same letter Montagu expressed succinctly the dangers to the Empire of this separate representation: 'We are riding two constitutional horses. From the back of the first we proclaim the unity of the Empire, from the back of the other horse we proclaim that the British Empire be represented by something like 14 representatives.' [15] (He meant two from each of the big Dominions and India, plus one from New Zealand, plus the Empire delegation itself). Events in Paris were to show the Dominions and India put their interests first and those of the Empire second. In the same letter Montagu revealed the interesting fact that belatedly the Indian National Congress had nominated Bal Tilak, the first advocate of *swaraj* (home-rule), as its nominee in Paris. 'We have refused passports and nothing has been done,' wrote Montagu dismissively.

'We have refused passports and nothing has been done'
EDWIN MONTAGU ON BARRING THE INC FROM THE PEACE CONFERENCE, 1919

7

India and the League of Nations

Long before the end of the First World War, statesmen had pondered over the setting-up of an assembly of the world's nations to try to make war impossible in the future, and this was the first major task to be undertaken in Paris. As the British diplomat Harold Nicolson put it: 'We journeyed to Paris not merely to liquidate the war but to found a new order in Europe. We were preparing not Peace only, but Eternal Peace.'[1] With hindsight, we must find this hopelessly utopian. In fact the League of Nations lasted for only twenty years before the Second World War showed how ineffective it had been. But we should not mock, for as its successor, the United Nations, shows it could only be as strong as the statesmen and citizens of the world wanted it to be. It was, said one of its architects, Lord Robert Cecil, 'a great experiment'. At its very last assembly he asked rhetorically: 'Is it true that all our efforts for those twenty years have been thrown away?' He answered himself: 'For the first time an organisation was constructed, in essence universal, not to protect the national interest of this or that country but to abolish war.'[2]

The leaders of the Great Powers all wanted a League of

Nations, but with reservations. President Wilson was the most morally committed but vague about the practice. Prime Minister Clemenceau said he 'greatly favoured such a League and he was prepared to make any sacrifice to achieve it',[3] but he did not really believe it was possible. Lloyd George added his endorsement: 'A League of Nations is an absolute essential to permanent peace and without peace we cannot have progress',[4] but in Paris he showed little interest in its construction.

The subject was discussed at the last meeting of the Imperial War Cabinet on Christmas Eve 1918. Here the Dominions showed their hand. Some leaders like Robert Borden of Canada and Jan Smuts of South Africa (though he did not attend the meeting) were enthusiastic; others, like Billy Hughes of Australia, were cynical; but all saw it as a great opportunity. Assuming the League was to endure, independent membership with the right to vote against Britain, if necessary, would be the strongest proof of self-government. To obtain an independent place in international negotiations rather than rank as a dependency without any existence in international law was a huge prize to be won. As Hughes said: 'It will be one of those questions at the Conference which would most vitally concern the Dominions.'[5] Of course, to be a Plenipotentiary Power at the Peace Conference was a major recognition in itself, but the Peace Conference would end when the Treaty was signed. Edwin Montagu shared the Dominions' view, later writing to Lord Chelmsford, 'I felt that as India was a nation for separate representation at the Peace Conference, it had got to be a separate nation in the League of Nations.'[6] Speaking as a loyal imperialist Montagu raised doubts about the viability of the Empire in such a world forum, but speaking as an advocate of Indian autonomy he saw the opportunity such a forum presented.

On 25 January the Plenary Conference in Paris formally approved a Covenant Committee, so called, to draw up a framework for a League of Nations. The 19 members met for the first time at the Hôtel de Crillon on 3 February. The British Empire delegation consisted of Jan Smuts and Robert Cecil. Both were true believers in a League of Nations and had already published their own proposals about the powers and practicalities of such a body. The chairman was President Woodrow Wilson, thereby imposing an impossible workload on himself, with Robert Cecil acting as his deputy. These two appointments were fortunate for India. The Covenant Committee met almost every day and, incredibly after only ten days work, prepared a draft Covenant or framework of the League of Nations for discussion at the Plenary Conference on 14 February. It was, as the first British history of the Peace Conference says: 'No result of laborious spade-work by expert sub-committees of the conference or protracted negotiation between heads of governments such as went to make up the other twelve chapters of the Treaty. We have, rather, a stroke of statesmanship, a rapid focussing of fragmentary studies and discussions into a reasonable scheme of preliminary organisation.'[7]

The questions that had to be answered were wide-ranging and profound, and the answers had to be arrived at without the benefit of public opinion or the luxury of much discussion, for Wilson was an impatient chairman. As Margaret MacMillan puts it: 'Should it be a policeman or clergyman? Should it use force or moral suasion? The French wanted a League with the power to stop aggressors by force. Lawyers in the English-speaking world put their faith in international law and tribunals. For pacifists there was still another remedy, general disarmament and a promise from all members of the

THE LEAGUE OF NATIONS

At the end of his massive *War Memoirs*, David Lloyd George wrote the League of Nations 'was the only hope of averting yet further and more terrible wars in the years to come'. He wrote the lines in 1936 when the Second World War was only three years away. 'Peace has seemed a sorry prize for so much blood and sweat,' he admitted. What were the constitutional weaknesses in the Covenant that rendered the League so fallible from the time it came into being in January 1920?

The first was the doctrine of national equality. Although the Covenant Committee had ignored the Japanese proposal for racial equality, the smaller nations would not allow any compromise with the equality of nations. Hence the Great Powers, fearing the others might get together and outvote them, insisted most League decisions in the General Assembly had to be unanimous. The same applied in the Council.

The second was the lack of sanctions. Although the French delegates made repeated attempts to set up some kind of international police force to supervise national armaments, they were overruled. Similarly, all League members pledged themselves to respect national boundaries and the independence of other states, but there was no League army to ensure they did so.

A crippling setback was the absence of key nations from the League in its early years. The Germans were not allowed to join until 1926 although they had signed the Treaty; they left in 1933. The Soviet Union was only admitted in 1934 and expelled in 1940. The United States never did join. When Wilson, architect of the League, returned home in 1919 he found a small group of Republican isolationists in the Senate against any further entanglement in Europe's future conflicts. Refusing to make any compromises himself he stumped the Union appealing to the people. In September he collapsed with a stroke on a night train and with his collapse went hopes of ratification. Although a large majority of Americans approved of the Covenant in principle, the Senate voted against ratification in March 1920.

The hopes of a new world order were condemned to frustration and defeat.

League to abstain from war. And what was the League going to be like? Some sort of superstate? A club for heads of state? A conference summoned whenever there was an emergency?

Whatever shape it took, it would need qualifications for membership, rules, procedures and a form of secretariat.'[8]

The Covenant Committee was pleased with its efforts. 'Many terrible things have come out of this war,' declared President Wilson on 14 February, 'but some very beautiful things have come out of it. A living thing is born, a definite guarantee of peace and a great humane experiment.'[9] However, several parties were absent from this 'humane experiment', for the defeated nations were not invited to join the League. Robert Cecil wrote ominously: 'The atmosphere of *Vae Victis* ['woe to the vanquished'] is not a good one in which to frame a lasting peace.'[10]

The first draft resolution of the League Covenant made no provision for separate Dominion representation, the result in part of the notion that the Empire should speak as one. Once again, it was pressure firmly applied by Borden and more erratically by Hughes that prevailed. The Supreme Council, consulted on matters of national controversy, formally concurred the Dominions had the same rights in these matters as other members of the League.

The position of India, however, was different. It was neither independent nor self-governing, and while this had not worried Lloyd George when he admitted India to the Imperial War Cabinet and thence to Plenipotentiary status at the Peace Conference, it did matter to Robert Cecil and others on the Covenant Committee. After all, Article 7 of the draft Covenant clearly stated 'admission to the League shall be limited to fully self-governing countries including dominions and colonies'. This was a wording, wrote Cecil to Bikaner with diplomatic tact, 'which taken by itself might give rise to apprehension in regard to India'.[11]

Montagu and Sinha were in London for the State Opening

of Parliament so the challenge of getting India into the League of Nations fell to Bikaner. On 2 February, when this anxiety first became apparent, he and Sinha both wrote to Montagu, putting forward the case for India's inclusion. Sinha's note made the legal point that India's Plenipotentiary status as 'a belligerent power with special interests' was *ipso facto* sufficient entitlement for membership in the League, like the Dominions proper. Bikaner spread himself in an unrestrained and indignant peroration that is worth quoting at length:

As the resolution [of 25 January] clearly states that the League should be open to every civilised nation which can be relied on to promote its objects, I would beg to point out that on this ground alone the claims of India for inclusion are unimpeachable. I would venture to urge with all the emphasis at my command that if the people of India with their ancient civilisation were considered fit to fight in Europe and in other theatres of the war side by side with the other nations of the world in this tragic drama, then on the grounds of civilisation and the still higher grounds of our common humanity there can be no just or cogent excuse to deny India her admission into the League.

The President of the United States of America stated that we were assembled to make the settlements made necessary by the war and also to secure the peace of the world. He laid stress on the fact that we were not representatives of governments but representatives of peoples and that we should satisfy the opinion of mankind. He also pointed out that the burdens of the war had fallen in unusual degree upon the whole population of the countries involved – upon older men, women and children; the strain of war had come from wherever the heart of humanity beats. Where it is a question of securing the peace of the world, the important fact must be borne in mind that India represents one fifth of the entire human race.

Lord Sinha has shown that India has been fully and ungrudgingly admitted to His Britannic Majesty's Government and to the inner councils of the Empire. India has also received special representation at the Council table of the Peace Conference. After having borne arms while freedom and civilisation hang in the balance, and having actually entered the portals of the peace temple, which in itself is a League of Nations, is India to be told to walk out as no longer belonging to the civilised nations of the world?

It is almost inconceivable that any of the other Powers should take up such an ungenerous and unjust attitude. We are certain that the British Government will never agree to the exclusion of India.[12]

> ... On the grounds of civilisation and the still higher grounds of our common humanity there can be no just or cogent excuse to deny India her admission into the League.
>
> **THE MAHARAJA OF BIKANER, 1919**

Faced with this broadside from the majestic Maharaja, who could offer resistance? In fact, at the meeting of the Covenant Committee on 5 February, Lord Cecil summed up the dilemma. On the one hand: 'India should be included in the League of Nations by virtue of the signature of the Covenant by representatives of the British Empire and in the view of the hope of President Wilson that India would be a member of the League.'[13] On the other hand, Article 7 expressly included only colonies with full powers of self-government. At that meeting the question was put on one side. It seemed quite possible to Montagu, at least, that India could still be excluded. He cabled Bikaner from London: 'I am a little disturbed on reading League of Nations Convention as to India's position and can only find comfort in the fact that you were good enough to charge yourself with personally watching this matter and you have not committed to me any anxiety. Would you see Lord Robert Cecil and let me know whether India is all right? If there is any anxiety I must see the Prime Minister before I return on Wednesday.' [14]

On 12 February, Bikaner wrote to Cecil for clarification. On 14 February, Cecil replied, after the Plenary Conference that day had considered again the draft Covenant's proposed Constitution of the League, including the status of India: 'The whole of this Article 7 with regard to admission is now confined to the case of states who are not signatories to the Covenant and not named in the protocol hereto as states to be invited to adhere to the Covenant. I have personally no doubt that India will be included as an original signatory and legal advice I have taken supports the view. I am quite sure that, especially in the view of the support promised by President Wilson, no objection would be raised to this course.' [15]

What had caused Cecil to make up his mind in favour of India's membership? Between these two meetings Bikaner had obtained an audience with the Supreme Council. Here he had won over President Wilson who was, most significantly, also the Chairman of the Covenant Commission. Later, Montagu described this audience in another letter to the Viceroy, not disguising his elation: 'He has covered himself in glory, gained the point, even bearding and obtaining the necessary answer from the great President Wilson himself! I am afraid there will be no holding him when he gets back to India! He appears to have finished his triumph by inviting Clemenceau to go and shoot tigers with him. That amazing septuagenarian has that one ambition, and you may find him in your jungles next cold weather. The whole proceeding appears to have concluded by

Bikaner displaying to the Big Five the tiger tattooed on his arm, which was inspected and approved not only by Clemenceau, but by Orlando and Wilson. Thus we make peace with Germany.'[16]

Proof of this endearing exhibitionism comes from Philip Kerr, Lloyd George's Private Secretary. On 22 February he wrote to the Prime Minister about a visit made by Balfour to Clemenceau, lying in his sick bed after he, 'the amazing septuagenarian', had been shot in the ribs by a madman in an assassination attempt on 19 February: 'He found him very fit. He says he expects to be in his office on Monday and back in the Conference on Wednesday. He told Mr Balfour with great glee that the Maharaja of Bikaner had asked him to go shooting tigers with him in India but this would now be unnecessary as he had since discovered there was tiger shooting in the streets of Paris.'[17] (Clemenceau's nickname was 'The Tiger' because he was ferocious when roused.)

> 'He appears to have finished his triumph by inviting Clemenceau to go and shoot tigers with him.'
>
> MONTAGU DESCRIBING BIKANER BEFORE THE SUPREME COUNCIL, 1919

'Le Tigre de France', as Bikaner called Clemenceau, took up the offer the following year, soon after he retired from office. He attended a *shikar* (a shoot) in Bikaner and bagged two tigers. After he returned home he wrote a 'thank you' letter that presumably was unreciprocated so he wrote again: 'I see you are not a great writer yourself, but I am not going to complain of it, my reason being that you are as near perfection as imperfection can be. Wherever you are, if you don't write a line I will call you a great prince but a naughty boy.'[18] The Maharaja was a popular character with a great capacity for friendship.

On 17 March Bikaner wrote a paper for the British Empire delegation: *We need hardly point out that India amply fulfils the condition of membership enunciated by President Wilson viz. that of being a civilised country which can be relied on.*[19] The Plenary Conference of 28 April finally ratified the revised Covenant, giving India the status of 'a self-governing State, Dominion or Colony'.

The India delegation was jubilant. On his way home to India on board the ss *Manora* in July, the Maharaja dictated to the Secretary of his Cabinet, Naunchal Singh, a statement about his role in Paris: *It fell to the lot of His Highness to conduct these negotiations single-handed, with satisfactory results. In this connection the Secretary of State for India wrote and telegraphed to His Highness congratulating and thanking him for the 'good service you have rendered to India'.* The start of the next paragraph is crossed out but it says, *As further recognition of His Highness's services to the Empire, His Imperial Majesty the King-Emperor was graciously pleased to confer the honour of G C V O* [Grand Cross of the Victorian Order] *on His Highness.*[20]

Montagu and Bikaner were elated by their successful negotiations, but the simple fact remained that India in 1919 was clearly not 'a self-governing State, Dominion or Colony'. When Robert Cecil wrote his own history of the League of Nations in 1941, *A Great Experiment*, he referred to India's anomalous status: 'In fact she was at that time controlled through the India Office by the United Kingdom Parliament and in the last resort India would have been bound to vote and act at Geneva [where the League of Nations was based] in accordance with the views of the English Cabinet [*sic*]. This anomaly was recognised and discussed in our Commission. But no serious objection was taken to it.'[21] The serious objection would come two years later, from the 'English Cabinet'. It was an anomaly that would cost Montagu his job as Secretary of State for India.

While the Dominions and India were united over the need for separate representation in the League, they were deeply divided over the proposed 'racial equality clause' in the Covenant. The Founding Fathers of America regarded it as a self-evident truth 'that all men are created equal' (Declaration of Independence, 1776). Self-evident it may be, but in 1919 the statesmen of the world found this a highly contentious issue. The Japanese delegation proposed such a clause and it provoked embarrassment, philosophical rumination and downright anger.

The Japanese people were infuriated they were not allowed to settle freely on the West Coast of America or in Australia, so when their delegate, Baron Makino, proposed such a clause for the Covenant, the Australians put word around Paris their real aim was to enable this over-populated nation to settle anywhere round the Pacific. Prime Minister Hughes was furious: 'Our White Australia policy would be a pricked bladder. Our control of immigration laws would be so much waste paper.' [22] He and others saw an inevitable spread of 'the Yellow Peril'. Baron Makino assured the Covenant Committee on 13 February the Japanese wanted only to establish the principle and each nation could work out its own policy. He simply wanted an extension to the proposed Article 21 that said: 'The High Contracting parties agree that they will not prohibit the free exercise of any creed, religion or belief whose practices are not inconsistent with public order and no person shall be molested in life or liberty by reason of his adherence to such creed, religion or belief.' [23]

Why not, said Baron Makino ingenuously, apply this

principle to race? Was not the League itself a family of nations? Specifically he proposed: 'The equality of nations being a basic principle of the League of Nations, the High Contracting Parties agree to accord, as soon as possible, to all alien nationals of states members of the League, equal and just treatment in every respect, making no distinction, either in law or in fact, on account of their race or nationality.'[24] But the principle itself was inflammatory. The White Dominions, by definition almost, were racist. Could they claim to regard their indigenous peoples as equal? – the Inuit in Canada? the Bantu in South Africa? the Aborigines in Australia? the Maoris in New Zealand?

The Europeans took a more sophisticated view that nevertheless reflected the prejudice of the age. The British Foreign Secretary, Arthur Balfour, murmured he found the proposition of equality interesting but he did not really believe it – you could scarcely say a man living in Central Africa was equal to a European. Lord Cecil realised the 'racial equality clause' was bound to cause trouble. It had, he said in that meeting on 13 February, already caused problems among the British Empire delegation. He suggested postponement of the issue and the draft Covenant went forward without the proposed Article 21.

The Japanese, however, would not give up. Their press was bitter about the 'so-called civilised world', and with reason. Hughes wrote in his autobiography that the evening before the meeting of the Covenant Committee on 11 April, the Japanese Plenipotentiary Baron Makino came to see him 'beslobbering me with genuflexions and obsequious deference'[25] to say he had persuaded both Smuts and Cecil to vote for the racial equality clause the next day. Hughes saw danger. Aware Wilson needed votes from the US West Coast to get the overall

League package through Congress, he worked on the hostile American press through the night by telephone, stirring up its xenophobic fears. The next day one of the less glorious meetings of the Covenant Committee took place.

Baron Makino made his proposal, though toned down to specify 'equality of nations' rather than of race. Cecil backed away from supporting the clause on the grounds that although he agreed with it, it 'encroached on the sovereignty of states and interference in their domestic affairs'. According to David Hunter Miller, a professional drafter attached to the American delegation who was at the meeting, 'it seemed to me at the time that Cecil felt he was performing a disagreeable duty. After making his statement he sat with his eyes fixed on the table, and took no part in the subsequent debate.'[26] The other British Empire delegate on the Covenant Committee, Jan Smuts of South Africa, was absent, perhaps conveniently. Nevertheless, a majority of the Committee wanted to vote for an amendment, so Chairman Wilson was left in a difficult position. He tried to extricate himself by expressing complete agreement with the Japanese that 'the equality of nations was a fundamental principle of the League of Nations' but then admitted that it 'perhaps would not be wise to insert such a provision' because it would cause 'the greatest difficulty'. In other words, it was too controversial! The committee then insisted on a vote and 11 out of the 17 members voted in favour. Wilson refused to accept the vote because decisions of the Committee had to be unanimous (this was disputed) and 'there were serious objections on the part of some of us'.[27] This was a clear reference to Cecil. The matter was then dropped, perhaps leaving a bad taste in the mouth of those assembled to create a new and better world. Afterwards Lord Cecil made the oracular observation: 'It is better that the Covenant be silent on these questions of right. Silence would avoid much discussion.' [28] The truth was the British Empire delegation had effectively scuppered the 'racial equality clause'.

Makino raised the race issue one more time, at the Plenary Conference on 28 April that approved the revised Covenant. Once more he referred to the 'equality of nations' and omitted mention of race. His speech went unheeded although he emphasised once again he was only interested in the principle; Japan had no intention of insisting on the practice in any specific context. He warned the failure of the League to agree on the basic right of racial equality boded ill for the future. He was right. But there was no discussion and the Conference moved on to other matters.

> 'It is better that the Covenant be silent on these questions of right. Silence would avoid much discussion.'
>
> ROBERT CECIL ON THE DEBATE ABOUT RACIAL EQUALITY, 1919

We know that Bikaner and Sinha approved of the racial equality clause behind the scenes, had done so from the start, and dissented from the views of the White Dominions. We can only guess at their strength of feeling. Proud of the ancient civilisation of India, and disgusted by the current racial prejudice in the British press against the Government of India Bill, they must have held many uncomfortable arguments over these two months. The Maharaja must have found Billy Hughes – 'I would walk into the Seine, or the *Folies Bergeres* with my clothes off [rather than accept the clause]' [29] – hard to take. The only written evidence for this, however, comes in the minutes of the British Empire delegation meeting on the eve of the Plenary Conference on 28 April. During a discussion on the proposed Japanese 'declaration' for racial equality, Lord Sinha said bravely if it were discussed 'he would be obliged to come forward in the Plenary Session in support of the Japanese position'.[30] The Maharaja was at the meeting but his views were not recorded.

The League of Nations was based on humanitarian ideals although they were compromised in practice. It was the same with the International Labour Organisation commissioned by the Peace Conference on 25 January 1919. Here, however, the Indian delegation acted against the ideals although with the best of intentions. The first three decades of the 20th century witnessed the rise of political parties representing the new power of labour, the growing masses of 'cloth-cap' workers in industry. Socialist parties and trade unions held frequent international meetings in Europe to lay down rules governing working conditions. So the Commission on Labour Legislation set up at the Peace Conference (first under the chairmanship of Samuel Gompers, head of the American Federation for Labour and then under George Barnes, a leading Labour MP who served in Lloyd George's Coalition Cabinet), was nothing new – except Germany was admitted to membership. It was not difficult for the Commission to agree on the general ideals of working conditions – for a maximum eight-hour day, against child labour – but it was impossible to give practical effect to these, bearing in mind the huge range of living standards and industrial progress in the different nations. This was where India demanded a voice.

India was not an industrialised nation in 1919. Its leaders complained this was partly because it had to tolerate the economic policies of the mother country, Britain, which were

> '[I] would be obliged to come forward in the Plenary Session in support of the Japanese position.'
>
> SP SINHA SUPPORTING RACIAL EQUALITY, 1919

in favour of free trade and importing raw materials to feed its own industrial might. Sinha spoke bluntly to the London Chamber of Commerce in 1918: 'Rich in all the resources of nature, India continues to be the poorest country in the civilised world. The industrial development of India is the most essential need of the present moment. Without an increase of prosperity it is useless to expect India to remain loyal within the Empire. Literally millions of Indians are on the border of starvation. What is wanted is a democratic government with the right to intervene against the exploded ideas of laissez faire. The development of commerce must come from protecting our weak industries against British imports, particularly of cotton.'[31]

He was simply voicing what the INC wanted: *swadesh* or economic self-sufficiency. Indian industry needed to impose tariffs to keep out foreign industrial imports. Demonstrating how serious an issue this was, in 1917 the British Indian Government had agreed to take over £100 million of Britain's war debt in exchange for the right to tax Lancashire cotton. By 1919, war inflation and rising prices (up 50 per cent since 1914) had brought about an economic depression. This was simply not the time to limit the employment of men, women and children on humanitarian grounds.

Both Sinha and Bikaner spoke against the Charter of Labour at that first Plenary Session. The Maharaja used an argument that could have had dangerous repercussions because he demanded exclusion, not inclusion, for the Princely States: *As the territories of the Ruling Princes lie outside British India and as legislation enacted for British India cannot apply to Indian States, and as furthermore the only competent authority to legislate for an Indian State is the Government of the State concerned, it should be clearly understood that the authority within whose competence the matter lies for enactment of legislation is the constituted authority of the Indian State concerned.*[32]

The Indian delegation was not the only one to object. It became clear that provision had to be made to enable 'backward' countries to assist in the drafting of legislation without the requirement to carry it out straight away. This time the Japanese delegation came up with an elegantly worded compromise: 'In framing any recommendation of general application, the Conference shall have due regard to those countries in which climatic conditions, the imperfect development of industrial organisation or other circumstances make the industrial development substantially different, and shall suggest modifications which meet the case of such countries.'[33]

The first British history of the Peace Conference concludes: 'In the terms as finally settled due allowance was made for the needs of India and Japan in this regard.'[34] No doubt because the Commission on Labour Legislation made such sensible compromises and worked away as a side-show, its recommendations were accepted without further fuss. The International Labour Organisation held its first meeting before the end of 1919 and it continues to exist today, under the umbrella of the United Nations, specialising in the Fundamental Principles and Rights at Work.

8

The Paris Peace Conference – India and the Ottoman Empire

How did the members of the Indian delegation spend their time during the five months of the Paris Conference between 12 January and 28 June 1919? After all, the Plenary Conference only met formally on six occasions and the Indian delegation only met with the Supreme Council over two issues, membership in the League and 'the Turkish Question'. The answer is that SP Sinha was over in London for much of the time steering through the Government of India Bill, and Edwin Montagu was sitting on a Committee of Experts recommending how much reparation Germany should pay for starting the war. That left Bikaner, characterised unfairly by Margaret MacMillan as the Maharaja 'who liked dinner parties and said little'.[1]

He certainly did like social occasions and there was plenty of scope for them in Paris, the centre of the world for these heady few months. The Hotel Majestic buzzed with excitement and gossip and hosted a full social schedule: dances at least every Saturday night when single women wandered freely between rooms, for few diplomats had brought their wives; amateur theatricals during the week; and dinner party after dinner party. The Maharaja kept large files for 'Invitations Accepted' and 'Invitations Declined', an example of the former being a dinner with Lloyd George in May when he and the Aga Khan tried to persuade the British Prime Minister to make Montagu the next Viceroy. Bikaner spent some time in London too, using as addresses the Carlton Hotel in Pall Mall and 41 Sloane Street.

There was plenty of work demanding attention from such a conscientious ruler, both in regard to India and for the Peace Conference. In his absence the Maharaja had been voted Secretary of the Princes Conference once again, and between 6 and 20 June he was summoned to London to attend meetings at the India Office about the Constitution of the Chamber of Princes. Despite his official position, as the only Indian present he raised eyebrows there and in India about whose side he was on. In his file at the Lallgarh Palace are 89 notes he dealt with in Europe concerning the administration of Bikaner during this period. Prominent among these were discussions about sending the *Ganga Risala* (his Camel Corps) to help quell the disturbances in Afghanistan and further negotiations about the Gang Canal. Once again, the Maharaja's displeasure at the interference of the Government of India came to the surface: *I strongly object to the Government of India approving of the arrangements I made for conducting the administration of the state during my absence and also to their asking that the Political Agent should be kept informed of all matters of importance during my absence. It is an infringement of my full sovereign powers and interference in the internal affairs of my state.*[2]

The Maharaja also had to deal with dozens of 'Top Secret' documents from the British government. There were thousands of dense pages to be read on such matters as the Future Strength of the German Fleet, the Kiel Canal, and the Teschen Commission on the International Boundaries of the Czechs and Poles. No wonder the Maharaja wrote to one of the Ruling Princes on 22 April: *My dearest Bhai, Please God I hope you are well. We are feeling well but long to return home. We feel your Olun* [a Marwari poetic term for 'constant thinking of the absent one'] *also very much. It is very satisfactory to find that the claims of the Indian States to special representation have been recognized. It is still too early to say when the signing of the Peace will take place but all the people of Europe want Peace quickly. Then, please God, we shall be able to leave at once for India, perhaps in May, and then your nephew and I will be shooting your tigers at Chitranasi before the rains.*[3]

A story still told in Bikaner is when Lord Chelmsford asked the Maharaja what he would like as a reward for his services during and after the war, he replied 'Mesopotamia'. The Viceroy replied tactfully this was out of his control. In the end, the Maharaja settled for the following as war booty: two aeroplanes, two Turkish guns, seven machine guns and 51 assorted rifles as well as many swords and pistols; and many decorations as well.

In 1919, the land of Mesopotamia was occupied by British and Indian troops; the river Tigris was patrolled by the British navy; and the country was administered by the India Office, prior to agreement about its future. Lloyd George wanted to set up an Arab state but to keep it under ultimate British control, and at first none of the other Great Powers dissented. Unlike Lloyd George, Clemenceau did not predict the future value of the recently discovered oil ('when I want some oil, I'll find it at my grocer's,' he said famously),[4] nor had he any interest in safeguarding the overland route to India. However, the future of Mesopotamia was part of an overall peace treaty settling the fate of the Ottoman Empire, and this was the last to be signed.

Although Lloyd George had predicted that this peace treaty would take about a week to draw up, it took 16 months from the first informal talks between Lloyd George and Clemenceau just after the armistice to the eventual signing of the Treaty of Sèvres in August 1920. During this period Allied troops enforced the armistice and nearly one million British soldiers were scattered over once Ottoman lands. Constantinople was divided into spheres of influence among British, American, Italian and French troops. The discussions in Paris between January and June 1919, therefore, were unfinished business. Yet they were negotiations in which the Indian delegation had a vested interest and a nagging voice. The issue was not Mesopotamia but Turkey itself, in particular the fate of the Sultan and Caliph, Mehmed VI, and of his capital, Constantinople. It was the only territorial and political matter in which India did have a say before the Supreme Council, and it caused severe unhappiness leading to threats of resignation.

On 5 January 1918 Lloyd George had made his keynote speech about 'war aims'. He had said about the Ottoman Empire: 'We do not challenge the maintenance of the Turkish Empire in the homelands of the Turkish race, with its capital in Istanbul – the passage between the Black Sea and the Mediterranean being internationalised and neutralised – but Arabia, Armenia, Mesopotamia, Syria and Palestine are, in our judgement, entitled to recognition of their separate national conditions.'[5] Yet when the Supreme Council began to discuss the matter on 30 January 1919, it seemed to many of those gathered in Paris, not least to the Indian delegation, that Lloyd George did not restrain his well known anti-Turkish and anti-Muslim prejudices. He adopted the Foreign Office view held since the days of Prime Minister William Gladstone that Turkey had no right to be in Europe but he added an invective of his own, first voiced with vehemence at the start of the First World War: 'The Turks are a human cancer, a creeping agony in the flesh of the lands which they misgovern, rotting every fibre of life ... I am glad that the Turk is to be called to final account for his long record of infamy against humanity.' [6] In Paris there was talk of internationalising Constantinople, perhaps of putting it under an American 'Mandate',

> 'Let us not, for Heaven's sake, tell the Muslim what he ought to think, let us recognise what they do think.'
>
> MONTAGU TO THE BRITISH CABINET, 1919

and of reducing the Sultan to a puppet potentate; or even kicking him out altogether. This is where the Indian delegation became alarmed. Upset no one seemed interested in Turkish opinion, Montagu pleaded with Balfour: 'Let us not, for Heaven's sake, tell the Muslim what he ought to think, let us recognise what they do think.' To which Balfour replied icily: 'I am quite unable to see why Heaven or any other power should object to us telling the Muslim what he ought to think.' [7]

Since the start of the war the India Office had been anxious about the loyalty of India's 60 million Muslims, aware they were at war against the titular head of their faith – for the Sultan of the Ottoman Empire and the Caliph, spiritual leader of Islam, were one and the same. These fears had proved much exaggerated, or at least buried, but now they came to the surface. In 1919 an All-India *Khilafat* (*sic*) Committee was formed in India to persuade the British to keep

Mehmed VI as world leader of Sunni Islam. This was its specific aim, for a wide range of Muslim opinion had watched in dismay as 'infidels' dismembered the Ottoman Empire and talked of taking over the Holy Places of Islam.

However, the philosophy of the *Khilafat* Movement was much broader. It looked back to the earliest days of Islam when the Prophet Muhammad was both spiritual and temporal leader of Islam and, viewed with the unquestioning nostalgia of the *Khilafat*s, led a land of democracy and purity. The movement, then, was a quest for an ideal higher than what its members saw as Western racism and imperialism. The All-India *Khilafat* Committee turned this idealism into utopian aims. Although Muslims in India were divided by language and custom and scattered over the subcontinent, it wanted Muslims to have their own laws, courts and education system separated from Hindu India. Not that Gandhi was without his own utopian vision, for his philosophy of self-sufficient village communities was not dissimilar. As with Gandhi, so the leaders of the *Khilafat* Committee stiffened

THE CALIPHATE
In early and medieval Islam, the Caliph (from the Arabic *khilāfa*, hence *Khilafat* movement in India) was the political and spiritual leader of the Muslim *ummah* or brotherhood – the successor of the Prophet Muhammad who died in 632. After his death, successive Caliphates were held by various dynasties, including the Umayyads of Damascus, the Abbasids of Baghdad, the Fatimids of Cairo and finally the Ottomans of Constantinople until Mustafa Kemal (later Atatürk) abolished the Caliphate in 1924. In its early days the Caliphate represented the ideal state of Islam, but it soon became neither ideal nor united. Long before the 20th century the Caliph was but a figurehead.

their utopianism with a dose of pragmatism when it came to turning on the British Raj. Indeed, Hindus and Muslims supported each other's campaigns although they were mutually opposed.

On 1 January 1919, leading Muslims in Europe like the Aga Khan wrote to Balfour demanding Turkey should remain an Islamic state, but their plea seemed to fall on deaf ears. Supporters of the *Khilafat* Committee began to fear their faith was imperilled. Their fear was stoked up outside and inside India by political forces. Through Afghanistan, once again embroiled in frontier wars, Bolshevik Russia spread the message of revolt. In Merv, in the Bolshevik Islamic Republic of Turkmenistan, a Turkish agitator preached 'Oh working Muhammadans! The Soviet Government has been formed to free you all. The British Government has enslaved the Muslims of India and dismembered the Turkish Empire.'[8] This was a new version of the Great Game. Inside India, Hindu nationalists expressed their sympathy and joined forces with the *Khilafat*s to stir up more trouble. Pamphlets appeared: 'The children of Islam, everywhere, are one and undivided. From China to Morocco, the Muslim world throbs with one feeling. The slightest injury to one part of this great spiritual organism touches its remoter part with poignant emphasis.'[9]

THE GREAT GAME
The term used for the strategic rivalry and conflict between the British Empire and the Russian Empire for supremacy in Central Asia, extending across the Himalayas to India, which continued after the Bolshevik Revolution. The phrase was given a popular and romantic meaning by the British novelist Rudyard Kipling in his novel *Kim* (1901). The Russian equivalent for 'The Great Game' is the 'Tournament of Shadows'.

On 20 March Bikaner received a formal letter from the leaders of the All-India *Khilafat* Committee demanding that full and independent control of the Holy Places of Islam should be left to the Khalifa (Caliph) of the Prophet (Sultan Mehmed VI) and that Constantinople must remain one of the Sultan's possessions. He sent it on to Lloyd George and raised the issue at the meeting of the British Empire delegation on 3 April. It was Montagu, however, who did most of the talking. He said Indian 'Mohammedans' (*sic*) were becoming 'increasingly apprehensive at the anti-Mohammedan policy of the Conference' and their loyalty should not be taken for granted. He described the battlefield scenes in Mesopotamia where 'after an attack against the Turkish forces, Indian Mohammedans would return to spread their prayer-carpets and pray for the well-being of the Sultan of Turkey'.[10] (One wonders how true this was.) His plea fell on deaf ears. It was not a matter that concerned the other delegates, and the Prime Minister was not moved.

The British were cynical about the motives of the *Khilafat* Committee. Did Indian Muslims really regard the weak and ingratiatingly pro-British Mehmed VI as their spiritual leader? Did they really think the Ottoman Empire, shortly to be dismembered, could be re-united spiritually? The young diplomat Harold Nicolson wrote: 'Our India Office is nervous over the Khalifat [*sic*]. I do not think our Indian Muslims care a hoot about it. What they like is to exercise pressure upon the British Government on behalf of the soldiers of Islam.'[11]

The India Office continued to be nervous. Montagu wrote to Lord Willingdon, Governor of Madras, on 16 April: 'The more news I receive from Upper India the more clear does it become that Moslem feeling is the real cause of the trouble, and in existing conditions of world politics it is difficult to see how anything substantial may be done to allay the disquietude which anticipations as to the fate of Turkey have provoked. I have done all I can in Paris and here to make the Indian Moslem point of view known to those in authority. Unfortunately, the fate of Turkey depends not on an Indian Secretary but on the balancing of all the views of all the Powers interested in the future disposition of this world.'[12]

Bikaner and Sinha, both Hindus, were in a difficult position. They could be accused of indifference, or even hostility, with harmful repercussions back home. So Bikaner wrote to Montagu: *I wish it were possible for a public statement to be made authoritatively announcing to the Muslim world in India that you, Lord Sinha and I have constantly kept the Muslim standpoint in view and that we have to the utmost of our ability and energy been pressing the Muslim case.*[13]

There is no reason to doubt his sincerity. In fact shortly afterwards the Maharaja was so goaded by what many saw as underhand and anti-Muslim diplomacy by the British government that he threatened to resign. On 6 May Lloyd George persuaded his Big Three colleagues, Wilson and Clemenceau, to allow the Greeks to reclaim their former territory of Smyrna on the Turkish mainland, thus precipitating what some saw as a Christian versus Muslim holy war. This was to have wide-ranging consequences. In the immediate term, Bikaner protested with vehemence. The Indian delegation circulated a memorandum stating Turkey was being treated more severely than Germany and that Lloyd George had broken his statement of intent of 5 January. It seemed as if the British Empire with its large Muslim population was, in Montagu's words, 'embarking on a campaign that was not merely anti-Turkish but anti-Mohammaden'.[14]

These were not propitious circumstances for the Indian delegation to have their audience before the Supreme Council, but it took place on 17 May. In fact only two days before a Greek force had invaded Smyrna leaving over 300 Turks and 100 Greeks dead. Black flags were flying in the streets of Constantinople. After the audience Montagu wrote to Lord Willingdon: 'Bikaner, Sinha and I had our audience with the Great Four last Saturday, and as it was clearly desirable that we should be accompanied by some Indian Mohamadens, I took along with me the Aga Khan [leader of the Muslim Ismaili sect] and Yusuf Ali [a famous Islamic scholar who translated the Koran into English and was known for his support of the Empire in the First World War]. We stated our case and were listened to with attention. What the result will be is not yet known, but I can fairly claim that as far as the Indian delegation is concerned, we have left nothing undone to bring the point of view of the Indian Mohamaden home to the powers that be.' [15]

In fact the delegation impressed Lloyd George. He pronounced: 'I conclude that it is impossible to divide Turkey proper. We would run too great a risk of throwing disorder into the Muslim world.' [16] If only he had heeded his own advice then his own Premiership and Montagu's political career may not have ended as prematurely as they did. But that is for the future. Meanwhile, on 21 May, Lloyd George and Clemenceau rowed over the future of Mesopotamia (Clemenceau had belatedly come round to realising the future value of oil), and already in Smyrna the conflict appeared out of control.

Negotiations about the future of the Ottoman Empire were put on hold. For the time being it was clear everybody trying to find answers to the Turkish Question had had enough. Montagu wrote to the Viceroy on 28 May: 'The ineffable delays, the flopping about, the changes in the Turkish peace cause me despair.' [17] Bikaner wrote home in early June: *God knows when we will, please God, reach India. We are quite fed up and longing to get home and see the family.*[18] In any event, what really mattered was whether Wilson's half-hearted offer to provide an American Mandate to govern Constantinople and the sea routes round it would be accepted by the American public, and this needed a vote in Congress.

Meanwhile, Bikaner reported in the same letter, the Allies had agreed on the German peace terms: *The German peace delegates are expected here on the 28th. It cannot be said when we will finish with them. They may sign at once, or after a week or two's delay, or refuse altogether to sign our terms. In the latter eventuality (which I do not think is impossible) it remains to be seen what we shall do – occupy Berlin, partition Germany, it cannot be foreseen. But I do not think the Germans are in a position to fight us again.*[19]

> It remains to be seen what we shall do – occupy Berlin, partition Germany, ... But I do not think the Germans are in a position to fight us again.
>
> THE MAHARAJA OF BIKANER, 1919

So the final act of the Peace Conference was staged in the Hall of Mirrors in the Palace of Versailles on 28 June. The German delegates had been summoned to hear their fate, not discuss it. They signed, pale and cowed, followed by the Allied leaders and Plenipotentiaries. An eyewitness wrote: 'The atmosphere of hate was terrible.' He described the order of signing: 'Then came Wilson (and his Plenipotentiaries), Lloyd George, who smiled broadly as he finished, the Colonial Premiers, and the Maharaja of Bikaner, looking magnificent in a pale khaki turban. After that Clemenceau ... .'[20] For this reason, the Maharaja of Bikaner's signature on the Treaty of Versailles comes immediately above that of Prime Minister Georges Clemenceau, the Chairman of the Conference. The subject of LS Rathore's biography of Maharaja Ganga Singh of Bikaner lived up to its title, *The Regal Patriot*: 'Tall, handsome, with thick dark moustache, glowing with pride over his youthful appearance, the Maharaja of Bikaner, who was wearing a traditional dress, appeared splendid and regal as he put his signature on the Treaty.'[21]

The Maharaja wasted no time leaving Paris. He cabled home: *Peace signed today with Germany. Starting for Marseilles. Sailing tomorrow, twenty-ninth. Maharaja.* On the voyage home on the ss *Manora* he dictated to his secretary: *It was thus for the first time in Indian history that the signature of an Indian Prince representing the Princes of India appeared on a document the most fateful in the history of the world and which, it is earnestly hoped and prayed, will result in a stable and lasting peace.*²²

> The signature of an Indian Prince ... [has] appeared on a document the most fateful in the history of the world.
>
> THE MAHARAJA OF BIKANER, 1919

Montagu's view of Bikaner's contribution was somewhat deflating. He wrote to Lord Willingdon on 25 June: 'Bikaner returns home on Saturday night. I shall really miss him very much. He is a good fellow and a good friend and has done his very best to be of assistance.'²³

A keen huntsman, the Maharaja of Bikaner and his grandson Prince Karni Singh stand with their trophy, a blackbuck

III

The Legacy

After the peace treaties President Clemenceau travelled to India in 1923. He is photographed here at a tiger hunt with the Maharaja of Bikaner and the Maharaja of Gwalior

9

During February and March 1919, Montagu and Sinha had been over in London much of the time preparing to present a Bill to Parliament based on the Montagu-Chelmsford proposals of 1918. They knew that vicious opposition would come from the Tory right wing, in particular the Indo-British Association that regarded any reform as a sell-out of British power. In early March the Maharaja of Bikaner joined them as host of a dinner in honour of Lord Sinha at the Savoy Hotel. He took on the 'Die-Hards' without mincing his words: *Should reactionary influences prevail in wrecking or whittling down the reforms a situation of gravity will be created. The British Parliament should not accept the guidance of reactionaries whose constant libels are responsible in no small degree for the unrest in India. Let us not forget Edmund Burke's striking axiom 'a great empire and little minds go ill together'.*[1]

In fact the Government of India Bill met little opposition on its First Reading in May. Montagu wrote to the Viceroy: 'In the debate our opponents hardly showed their heads. I am a little puzzled by their silence.'[2] It was a different matter during the Bill's Second Reading on 5 June when the maverick Henry Page-Croft, MP for the short-lived Nationalist Party, spoke darkly about Montagu's 'oriental fervour' and 'revolutionary measures'.[3] By recruiting like-minded Tory MPs from a dinner he attempted a late-night filibuster, literally 'talking out a bill', intending that the House should break up for the summer recess without the Second Reading vote taking place. He was unsuccessful. Earlier in the debate Montagu had 'implored the House to show to India to-day that Parliament is receptive of the case of self-government'.[4] Most MPs did so. When the Bill reached Committee Stage the following October, poor Lord Sinha was ill with worry and went off to Harrogate to convalesce. The Government of India Act (1919) became law at the end of the year.

As we have seen, the world was a very different place in 1919 than it had been two years earlier. Revolutionary change was in the air, exemplified, of course, by events taking place in Paris. The world's economies were in recession, with subsequent social dislocation. A global influenza epidemic was killing no fewer than ten million Indians. No doubt this mood of unrest and fear increased the appeal of the *Khilafat* movement. On the North-West Frontier the Third Afghan War was tying down British Indian army troops. Fearing the worst, and aware that violence in India could arise convulsively, Viscount Chelmsford had set up a committee at the end of 1918 to investigate the likelihood of an uprising against British rule. The result was a number of pieces of legislation named after the British judge who chaired the committee, Sir Sidney Rowlatt. The Rowlatt Acts empowered the Raj authorities to imprison without trial any person suspected of terrorist activities. They came into effect in March 1919 and caused huge resentment. Although at the time Montagu gave them his reluctant support, they undoubtedly increased the civil unrest in north India. Gandhi, a former lawyer, saw them as a monstrous injustice and prepared for 'the greatest battle of my life'.[5] He called for an all-India *hartal* or suspension of work on 6 April, the first step in a campaign of *satyagraha*.

In the Punjab riots broke out in many towns that April. The Governor, Sir Michael 'Micky' O'Dwyer, who a few months earlier had called Montagu 'a knave' for his proposals of reform, saw them as the beginning of an insurrection to overthrow the Raj and determined on very heavy reprisals. He summoned a likeminded reactionary, Brigadier-General Reginald Dyer, to move his 45th Brigade to Amritsar. Here, it has to be said, severe riots had broken out after the arrest under the Rowlatt Acts of two Congress leaders who had organised the Gandhi *hartal*. When Dyer arrived on 11 April, he found that mobs carrying banners proclaiming 'The British Raj is at an End' had murdered three Europeans, molested an English woman (considered an heinous offence by the British) and fired Raj buildings. One hundred Europeans were cowering in the fort; the memory of the Indian Mutiny of 1857 must have been in their minds, and his. He determined on a condign punishment. Two days later he ordered his troops to mow down with rifle fire a peaceful demonstration of thousands of men, women and children who had gathered in an enclosed area with no way out. Three hundred and seventy-nine Indians were killed and 1,500 wounded.[6] Then Dyer ordered Indians to crawl past the spot where the English woman had been molested. O'Dwyer declared martial law throughout the Punjab. Gandhi, appalled by what he had unleashed, called off his *satyagraha* campaign on 18 April. The disturbances died down but bitter resentment remained.

To many British in India, the brutal actions of the British

army and police in the face of widespread riots in the Punjab prevented a second Mutiny and saved the Raj. To many Indians, the same brutal actions showed the inhumanity of the Raj and led justifiably to the mass movement for *swaraj* and *satyagraha*. Up against these extreme events, the new regional self-government in India and the status of India in the League of Nations were all but forgotten. What seems remarkable is that the progress of the India Bill through Parliament was not affected more by the riots and reprisals that were taking place in the Punjab. Today, with instant coverage on TV and the Internet, the terrible slaughter in Amritsar would have been on the minds of all MPs debating the future of India. Bikaner's fears, however, were to prove unfounded when he wrote home from Paris in April: *It is very sad to see these troubles breaking out. They strengthen the hands of the English extremists who will now have a new weapon to use against the reforms.*[7]

Montagu wrote to Chelmsford on 22 April: 'How suddenly the embers burst into flame, and how extraordinary widespread were the points at which the troubles broke out. Gandhi is a fanatic and I have no doubt he sincerely regrets having acted as he did. I was questioned in the House as to the cause of the troubles and I replied that there was no one cause. High prices, the Rowlatt Acts, the unrest that is so universal throughout the world, and, as regards the Mohammadens, alarm as to the fate of Turkey, all enter into the picture.'[8]

Chelmsford stuck by Dyer in public though in private he was appalled and wrote to Montagu: 'If only people would realise that the day has passed when you can keep India by the sword.'[9] Montagu wanted him recalled. Dyer himself remained convinced until the end of his days that he had saved the Punjab and hence the Raj from another mutiny, and many British at home and in India agreed with him. He repeated this before the Hunter Committee held a year later in India to enquire into the massacre. He was not believed. The Committee severely censured him and reprimanded O'Dwyer, as a result of which Dyer was recalled to England and forced into early retirement.

Such was the strength of feeling in his defence that when the findings of the Hunter Committee were debated in the House of Commons on 8 July 1920, members of the Indo-British Association almost attacked Montagu physically. 'Bolshevism' shouted a Tory MP. 'An Asiatic agitator' wrote *The Spectator*. Montagu repeated that the British could only hold India with the goodwill of its subjects and Lord Sinha said much the same thing in the House of Lords. It looked as if a rift was opening between radicals and reactionaries. That September, Montagu wrote to Lord Willingdon: 'I do not believe the Dyer incident was the cause of great racial exacerbation that is now in existence in India. As soon as the Indians were told we agreed with them and they were to become our partners, it instilled in their minds an increased feeling of insubordination. Similarly, when the Europeans were told that after driving the Indians for so many years, their regime was over and they had to co-operate with Indians, or even allow Indians to rule India, their race consciousness sprung up afresh. I am convinced this has been our fatal mistake. We ought to have let the Indians run their show from the beginning. We cannot remain in a country where we are not wanted, so we have either got to make our peace or get out of India and all its bother.' [10] This seems a sad conclusion from the man who only the previous year had been so proud of leading India through parliamentary reform and international treaty towards self-rule under the British Empire.

Montagu was also depressed that summer by the supposed resolution to the Ottoman question. In September 1920, the rump of the Sultan's government was forced to sign the Treaty of Sèvres, an unrealistic attempt to resolve the outstanding issues in favour of the Allies. The Americans were not signatories to the Treaty because they had withdrawn from peacekeeping after Congress had rejected the suggestion of a Turkish Mandate. The Treaty was never accepted by the new *de facto* ruler in Turkey, Mustafa Kemal, who had established a rival capital in Ankara and had been waging a war of national resistance to drive out the occupying armies for the last year. The Treaty had been imposed on Mehmed VI's impotent puppet government by the will of Lloyd George who, despite the opposition of his Cabinet, had insisted on Allied armies taking full control of Constantinople and pinning down Mustafa Kemal in Ankara, after which he announced 'Turkey is no more'.[11] It was too much for Montagu, who had a nervous breakdown. 'I hate it [the Turkish situation],' he wrote to Willingdon, 'but I find myself so hopelessly tired that there is positively nothing for me to do but acquiesce.'[12] The result of the Allied offensive was the Treaty of Sèvres, signed in a porcelain factory outside Paris on 10 August. In the neat phrase of Margaret MacMillan, the Treaty 'was not a thing of beauty but as easily smashed'.[13]

> 'We cannot remain in a country where we are not wanted, so we have either got to make our peace or get out of India and all its bother.'
>
> EDWIN MONTAGU, 1920

The Treaty of Sèvres was supposed to be the Versailles equivalent applied to the Ottoman Empire, but without the

MUSTAFA KEMAL ('ATATÜRK') (1881–1938)
He was a military genius who salvaged the Turkish nation from the disintegrating Ottoman Empire, resisting the occupying armies after 1918. He commanded the new state of Turkey as if it was the army and set it firmly on the road to westernisation. He believed Islam and the Ottomans belonged to the past. Hence he abolished the Caliphate, moved the capital to Ankara and turned the main mosque of Istanbul (Constantinople until 1930), Hagia Sophia, into a museum. In 1934 he was given the title of *Atatürk*, 'the Father of the Nation'. Now, both the reputation of Atatürk and his secular state are challenged in Turkey.

acquiescence of Mustafa Kemal, what did it mean? It did decide the future of Mesopotamia, which was to be 'provisionally recognised as an independent state ... advised and assisted' by the 'Mandatory Power' of Britain. This was less than the India Office had once wanted, but more than Britain could cope with. For years the new country (now Iraq) was beset by uprisings, bordering on anarchy, against the British-imported King Feisal, son of the Emir of Mecca. When the Mandate ended in 1932 and Iraq joined the League of Nations, the British heaved a sigh of relief.

Further west, the Turks surrendered the lands Lloyd George characterised tendentiously as lived in by 'non-Turkish populations', that is Smyrna, Thrace, Armenia and Kurdistan. Constantinople remained the Turkish capital due, it was rumoured, to Montagu's pleading with Lloyd George. The waters of the Bosphorus, the Dardanelles and the Sea of Marmara, known collectively as the 'Straits', were internationalised and the surrounding area, including Constantinople, was demilitarised. This meant its 'neutrality' was guaranteed by Allied troops, many of whom still patrolled the streets of the capital. Mustafa Kemal ignored the Treaty. Like the Russians resisting Napoleon in 1812 his army retreated

into the interior around Ankara, neither fighting nor surrendering. The Allied military advisers said it would take a
large army to quell the Nationalist resistance and only the
Greeks responded with force, though they were encouraged
and supported by British money. Initially the Greek army won
brilliant victories, but the Kemalist waves slowly gathered in
intensity and pushed back the Greeks from whence they had
come. The French recognised a winner, and made peace with
Mustafa Kemal that October.

Meanwhile a conference in London (February to March
1921) failed to renegotiate the Treaty of Sèvres sufficiently to
Kemal's advantage, and in early 1922 it became clear he was
planning a massive offensive in retaliation. Some 7,500 Allied
troops, mostly British, still patrolled the 'neutral' zone, and
now they were faced by a Turkish army of perhaps 50,000.
Another crisis was about to unfold that would bring down
Montagu and Lloyd George himself.

On 1 March 1922 the new Viceroy, Lord Reading, telegraphed to Montagu that the Muslims in India were dis-
tressed by the likelihood of a new war that would divide their
loyalties, and urged the British army to evacuate Constantinople and restore Smyrna and Thrace to the Turks. Lord
Reading wanted the telegram published and Montagu agreed,
although he had not warned the Cabinet. This played into the
hands of the 'Die-Hards' and Curzon, who accused Montagu
of breaking collective Cabinet responsibility. Lloyd George
sacked Montagu without more ado on 9 March. He had had
enough of his Secretary of State for India, ignoring the fact
he was also a member of the British government, though wise
constitutional hands like Robert Cecil had long seen that this
was a price to pay for giving India more autonomy when it
was actually governed by Britain. Lloyd George put it another

way. Irritated by Montagu's prickly nature and obsequious obstinacy he had written to him in 1919: 'In fact throughout the [Paris] Conference your attitude has often struck me as being not so much a member of the British Cabinet, but a successor on the [Mughal] throne of Aurangzeb.'[14]

Montagu mounted his familiar defence: 'India was given separate representation at the Peace Conference and was a party to the Treaty of Sèvres. Therefore I cannot conceive it possible that they [Indian Muslims] should not be allowed to express their views affecting the peace of India.'[15] This was a disingenuous, not to say clumsy, reply because the point was not whether Montagu had the right to speak for India but in what circumstances he should do so; but it did point up the conflict of interest.

LLOYD GEORGE ON MONTAGU, 1919

Events now moved towards a crisis. In September 1922, Mustafa Kemal's army slaughtered the Greeks in Smyrna (now Izmir). The 'Paris of the Levant' was put to the torch: 200,000 Greeks fled by ship. The Turkish army advanced on Chanak, where a small British garrison was holed up guarding the Dardanelles, and goaded the defenders by jeering at them across the barbed wire. On 29 September Lloyd George and Winston Churchill (until recently Secretary of State for War) telegraphed to the garrison that, 'unless his [the local Turkish commander's] troops are withdrawn at a time fixed by you, all the forces at our disposal, naval, military and air will open fire on the Turks.'[16] They had no Cabinet approval for what was, in effect, a threatened declaration of war, a war that very few in Britain or the Empire wanted.

It was the Chanak episode that ended Lloyd George's long Premiership. A future Prime Minister, Andrew Bonar Law, wrote to The Times saying that Britain could not act alone as 'the policeman of the world'.[17] The Conservative Party withdrew its support for the Coalition Government and Lloyd George was forced to resign on 19 October. He never held office again. Both sides were chastened by the realisation that a second world war could have been triggered, and in October a new armistice was signed. Immediately afterwards the Sultanate was abolished, and Mustafa Kemal was elected the first President of the new Republic. On 1 November Mehmed VI was smuggled out of Constantinople by the British in an ambulance with its red cross painted out (to avoid the charge of duplicity) and taken by British warship to Malta. He died in exile in San Remo in 1926. Finally, the weary diplomats gathered in Lausanne for one last treaty to wrap up the Ottoman Empire. The Treaty of Lausanne, signed in July 1923, gave Turkey the borders more or less that it has today. Curzon said: 'Hitherto we have dictated our peace treaties. Now we are negotiating one with an enemy who has an army in being while we have none, an unheard of position.' [18]

An epilogue remained. Although Mustafa Kemal was determined to create a secular state he did not feel powerful enough yet to abolish the seat of the world leader of Sunni Islam. The Assembly had appointed Mehmed VI's cousin, Abdülmecid II, as Caliph and he was a popular figure, for at this resurgent point in the nation's history he reminded citizens of the once-glorious Ottoman Empire. It was not to be. Only 15 months later, on 3 March 1924, Mustafa Kemal felt confident enough to have his way. The Caliphate was abolished and Abdülmecid was put aboard the Orient Express to live a life of exile in Switzerland. As the train sped past the site in Hungary where lies the heart of the greatest Ottoman ruler in history, Suleiman the Magnificent, he lamented, 'My ancestor came with a horse and flags. Now I come as an exile.'[19]

With the end of the Caliphate, the *Khilafat* movement in India collapsed. Its members merged into the Muslim League under Muhammad Ali Jinnah who, disapproving of Gandhi's campaign of *satyagraha*, had taken the League out of the INC in 1920. The seeds of Pakistan as an independent Muslim state may be traced back to this date. Co-incidentally, Edwin Samuel Montagu died the same year, in 1924, aged only 45.

10

Towards Independence: the Rise of the Congress Party

Sinha returned to India in 1920 as Governor of Bihar and Orissa, the first Indian to be promoted to the top of the British administration. Once again Montagu had to reassure Viscount Chelmsford that an Indian was capable of ruling India, but the truth was that by now Sinha was politically far more British than he was Indian. His views on eventual Indian self-government under the Raj expressed the official British position, while the Indian National Congress, of which Sinha had been President only five years before, had moved towards *swaraj* and *satyagraha*.

The new President in 1919 was Pandit Motilal Nehru (father of India's future Prime Minister) who was one of Gandhi's stalwart supporters. He backed Gandhi's plan of ordering the rank and file members of the INC to combat British rule directly by, for example, leaving their posts as government servants (October 1921), a move which if successful could have seriously embarrassed the Raj. Meanwhile Nehru's son, Jawaharlal, was touring Indian villages founding peasant's organisations called *kisans* and turning them against the British. By 1922, the *satyagraha* movement was out of the control of Congress. In February a mob wielding *swaraj* banners attacked a police station at Chauri Chaura, near Lucknow, and beat to death 22 policemen. Once again, as at Amritsar three years before, a violent incident caused Gandhi to recoil with self-questioning and the British to react with harsh measures. The Nehrus, father and son, had just been sent to prison and now Gandhi followed them, convicted of subversion. The balance of power in India had shifted towards the INC and now three years of civil disobedience were followed by five years of sullen obedience.

Sinha had no part in this. He held his post for nearly a year, but then resigned, pleading ill-heath. He did not have a strong constitution, but there were other reasons too. He was out of step with the times and he did not enjoy public administration. By training he was a lawyer who had only accepted political work and the accompanying honours out of a sense of duty. After a prolonged rest he returned to semi-public life with a series of articles for a Calcutta magazine called *The Bengalee*. In these he argued for patience and goodwill towards the British, but to little effect. By then he had returned to live in Britain where, in 1926, he became part of the legal establishment, a Bencher of Lincoln's Inn and a member of the Judicial Committee of the Privy Council. His last public act was to support the visit to India in 1928 of

THE NEHRU DYNASTY
Four generations of the Nehru family have dominated Indian political life over the last century. They are the nearest India gets to a political royal family. Pandit Motilal Nehru (1861–1931) was a leading freedom fighter. His son Jawaharlal (1889–1964) was India's first Prime Minister. His daughter, Indira Gandhi (1918–84) was Prime Minister twice before she was assassinated. Her son Rajiv (1944–91) succeeded her until he, too, was assassinated. His widow, Sonia (b. 1946) is still a leading member of the Congress Party.

the Simon Commission that was convened to report on the effectiveness of the Government of India Act to which Sinha had so substantially contributed. With crass insensitivity the Simon Commission did not include a single Indian, so Lord Sinha's support shows how far he was now assimilated into the British establishment. Forced to winter in India because of ill-health, he died at Berhampore (now in Bangladesh) on 4 March 1928. His friends said he embodied the best culture of East and West and bore his worldly success with modesty. His death at 65 saved him from having to confront the growing reality of Indian independence with the severance from Britain that required. His old friend the Maharaja of Bikaner was to find this deeply troubling.

After Gandhi was released from prison in 1924 he retreated to village life and preached the gospel of cotton-spinning as the means towards self-sufficiency. Jinnah spent most of the time at his legal practice in London. Then, in 1926, the British government re-galvanised the whole issue of Indian independence by forming the all-British Simon Commission. It seemed as if the INC was to have no part in India's future. The Nehrus, father and son, retaliated by passing two audacious motions at the 1928 Congress AGM, the first demanding Dominion status for India and the second demanding British withdrawal from India in a year's time if another bout of civil disobedience was to be averted. The Viceroy Lord Irwin accepted the first a year later, thereby implying Britain had given up any hope of retaining lasting authority over India, but of course he could not agree to the second, which was clearly blackmail. Its effect was counter-productive, anyway, because it raised the seemingly insoluble problem of giving the Hindus and Muslims the power and safeguards they both required.

The Nehru Report on the future of India, which was

commissioned by the INC in 1928, looked towards a federal government with a strong centre and no reserved seats for the Muslim community. (This is, in fact, what happened after 1947.) The Muslims saw this as a 'Hindu Raj' and Jinnah demanded not only the reservation of places for Muslims in both national and regional legislatures but also three designated Muslim states of Sind, Baluchistan and the North-West Frontier Province within a future Indian federation. The British government encouraged the two communities to negotiate, but when there was clearly an impasse it summoned all parties to a Round Table Conference in London, to take place towards the end of 1930. Congress resisted this, thinking rightly it would lose the initiative if it agreed. On 26 January 1930, known ever after as Independence Day, it launched another *satyagraha* for *swaraj*. Without the presence of the INC, the first Round Table Conference was bound to fail.

The undisputed leader of the Congress Movement was Gandhi, the semi-mystical but politically adroit *Mahatma* whom the peasants worshipped. Now he carried out a master-stroke of public relations. From his home in Ahmadabad he and his followers marched to the Gujarat coast 240 miles away, where salt had always been collected, as a symbolic gesture against the salt tax. The tax was in itself puny (only one and a half rupees a year) but it represented the power of the Raj over one of the essentials of Indian life. Thousands joined the march and the world's media watched with fascination. *Satyagraha* now spread, involving for the first time women and reaching south India. The British imprisoned thousands of Congress members, but still saw their power ebbing away.

The world's media were also outside the Viceroy's House in

Delhi in March 1931 to see Gandhi walk up the steps dressed in his peasant's cheap cotton *dhoti* (loin-cloth) to parley with the Viceroy himself. This was too much for Winston Churchill who called Gandhi 'that half-naked *fakir*' (holy man). Gandhi and Lord Irwin made peace so that another Round Table Conference could take place, this time with Gandhi present although Congress still pronounced it a 'sell-out'. Nevertheless, Congress temporarily called off its campaign of civil disobedience and the British released no fewer than 19,000 of its members from prison.

Gandhi returned from London empty-handed in 1932. Even he had been unable to solve the constitutional impasse between Hindus and Muslims. Civil disobedience broke out once more and the next Viceroy, Lord Willingdon, arrested 40,000 Indians over a three-month period. Gandhi was imprisoned again, for two years. Not that the British government was prepared to give up India immediately in any event. An India Defence League was formed with the old Rudyard Kipling as one of its vice-presidents (although in his famous poem 'Recessional' written in 1897 he had foretold the end of Empire) and Winston Churchill its most effective speaker. Churchill could not bring himself to accept the racial equality of Indians with the British nor their ability to govern themselves. The League mounted a formidable rearguard action with argument that went beyond India itself. 'England, apart from her Empire in India, ceases for ever to be a Great Power,' growled Churchill, echoing the words of Lord Curzon. Lord Rothermere, owner of the *Daily Mail*, saw India as belonging to England almost by divine right, so that if the British departed it would fall prey to communism and Russian invasion. India was wearing tempers thin and taking up too much of Parliament's time.

Nevertheless, the National Government decided on a new India Act in 1935. At provincial level it was a major advance on the Montagu-Chelmsford reforms. Now mostly Indian Ministers were to be responsible to their local legislatures for all branches of government, and the electorate was increased to 30 million Indians, one-sixth of the adult population. The INC saw this as a major opportunity, called off its *satyagraha*, and turned itself into the Congress Party.

Jawaharlal Nehru was clear about its intentions: 'We go to the Legislatures not to co-operate with the apparatus of British imperialism but to combat the Act and to seek to end it.'[1] In the 1935 elections it won nearly half the 1,500 seats in provincial legislatures, and formed governments in seven provinces, including Madras and Bombay. Predominantly Muslim parties won control of Lahore and the Punjab. However, once in power the provincial Congress Party governments did not try to 'end' the Act, but co-operated amicably enough with the British governors to whom they were answerable. What they did not do was allow power-sharing with the Muslim minorities in the five states where they had an absolute majority. The result was that far more Muslims joined Jinnah's Muslim League. His uncompromising view was that a united, independent India was only possible if Muslims were properly protected. The battle lines were well and truly drawn. The provinces, then, were on their way to independence but how united would they be at national level? Could they reach agreement as a 'federation' of states, forming a unity but remaining independent in internal affairs?

The Government of India Act (1935) stipulated Britain would retain control over the central government, in particular over defence and foreign policy, until one-half of the major princes in India agreed to its terms. The British government saw the princes as a device to diminish the squabbling between Hindus and Muslims and also minorities such as Anglo-Indians and Sikhs who had reserved seats in the Legislative Assembly. By 1935, however, the Indian princes were getting cold feet, aided and abetted by the Indian Defence League and British officials in Delhi who saw the opportunity of continuing British power and therefore their own for a little longer.

How did it come about that the Maharaja of Bikaner, once the leader of the Indian princes and also the champion of Indian autonomy, allowed his fellow princes to become a stumbling block to Indian independence? For that is what happened.

11
Towards Independence: Bikaner and the Fall of the Princes

The Maharaja had returned from Versailles covered in glory. He was elected the first Chancellor of the Chamber of Princes (COP) when the Duke of Connaught inaugurated it on behalf of King George V on 8 February 1921, according to the recommendations in the Government of India Act of 1919. This was no more than his due, for he had conceived and shaped it. For the next decade, at least, he dominated the princely states and was the India Office's favourite representative on international occasions. He attended the League of Nations in Geneva in 1924, and again in 1930 when he went on to London to address the Imperial Conference. Here he was the last of the old statesmen left, still looking majestic and speaking with succinct authority. Prime Minister Ramsay Mac-Donald told him afterwards: 'You were the doyen among the representatives present from every quarter of the Empire.' [1] There was even talk of him succeeding Lord Irwin as the next Viceroy.

The trouble was he could not resist playing the elder statesman, telling viceroys and his brother princes what to do. Although an impressive performer, he was increasingly brusque in his personal contacts. 'Bikaner was as usual ungracious and offensive,'[2] wrote O'Dwyer's Chief Secretary in 1926. Moreover, no prince was pricklier about his *izzat* or personal honour. He nearly walked out of a dinner hosted by the Prince of Wales because he was seated below the Maharaja of Patiala who actually shared the same number of gun salutes on his birthday as Bikaner, 17, the number that indicated rank in the princely hierarchy.

No one knew better than the Maharaja that the British government was devolving power in British India, and unless the COP acted effectively, its states would be left behind by the new India or increasingly threatened by it. There was growing antipathy between the princely states and the INC. Although Congress had not been able to extend its 'All India' *satyagraha* to the princely states, it did encourage the States' Subjects Conference, an increasingly powerful movement founded in 1929 with branches in many princely states that aimed to undermine the authority of the princes, chiefly in its early days by propaganda.

The India Office encouraged this confrontation because it saw the princely states as old India, 'Indian India', and used its increasingly out-of-date mantra of 'paramountcy' as a weapon to balance the old India with the new nationalism outside. Not surprisingly, therefore, the COP was preoccupied in determining its rights and obligations *vis-a-vis* the British government. In particular, what exactly did 'paramountcy' mean? And in this new era, did it make any difference that the princes were bound by treaty to the British Crown but not to the British government? In response to these questions posed by a Standing Committee of Princes that first met at Bikaner in 1926 to plan for the future, Lord Irwin asked Sir Harcourt

Butler, formerly Governor of United Provinces, to form his own committee and come up with some answers. In 1929 it reported unhelpfully that, in effect, British paramountcy must remain paramount.

The next year the Maharaja attended the first Round Table Conference in London on behalf of the princes. As we have seen, this was a forum to find a way forward for India but without the INC, which boycotted the proceedings. The leading Hindu delegate opened the case for the Indian nationalists by inviting the 'great princes of India to join hands with their brethren in British India' to establish an All-India Federation which would 're-unite the common motherland into a great nation'. In reply the Maharaja sprang to his feet and, to the surprise of almost everyone present, welcomed the proposition of federation: *I have for many years been a staunch believer in a federal constitution for India, which would unite as equal partners the states of India already sovereign, and the British Indian Provinces recently made autonomous. To this faith I adhere today.*[3]

This was indeed an alliance of convenience, because the COP mistrusted the intentions of the increasingly socialist INC, while many Congressmen thought the princes were so conservative they would even try to prevent the granting of Dominion status lest their own autonomy was threatened. Nevertheless, Bikaner was consistent with his long-held vision of a self-governing India, provided the rights of the princes could be guaranteed. To this end the Standing Committee of Princes, including Bikaner, had held discreet meetings on the subject with the Nehrus the previous year. Lord Irwin was upstaged and complained to the Secretary of State for India that Bikaner and other princes became 'obsessed with the hope and desire of eliminating paramountcy when

THE MAHARAJA OF BIKANER

they come to round table conferences'.[4] This was indeed an irony because Lloyd George had said much the same thing about Montagu when he came to the British Cabinet over Mesopotamia. Without the presence of the INC, the Round Table could only be a sounding board, and when Bikaner and the other princely delegates returned home they found some of their fellow princes as defensive as ever.

The Maharaja of Bikaner must have felt like Sisyphus. His labours continually returned the rock to the bottom of the hill. He became testy and disheartened. The COP had major internal weaknesses too. From the start the two big states of Hyderabad and Mysore would have no part in it. The small states did join, but many of them were concerned only with their own autonomy, however feudal this was, and responded with rudeness to any kind of interference. In vain did Bikaner try to define the standards without which a princely state did not deserve to survive in this highly political new India. He listed his *minima* as an independent judiciary, the rule of law, and security of life and property. In fact, Bikaner represented the mainly Rajput, 'middle-rank' Maharajas, those who spoke English, lived within motor transport of Delhi and moved with the times. He was related by marriage to several of them – the princely dynasties of Cutch, Kota Jodhpur, Kishengarh and others that guaranteed him a block of Rajput votes in the Chamber. Their members of the COP were less sophisticated and more conservative. n 1934 Bikaner, still a leader but no longer the Chancellor,

> I have for many years been a staunch believer in a federal constitution for India, which would unite as equal partners the states of India already sovereign, and the British Indian Provinces recently made autonomous.
>
> THE MAHARAJA OF BIKANER, 1930

threatened to resign unless the COP was more united; but it made little difference.

By the time of the Government of India Act of 1935, the Maharaja of Bikaner was 57. He had aged visibly in recent years, although he was still vigorous. He no longer commanded all and sundry with his regal presence and, worse, he had become a bit of a joke. The new Secretary of State for India, Lord Zetland, described him cruelly to the Viceroy Lord Linlithgow as an 'out-of-date windbag'.[5] Perhaps the Maharaja realised his days as a princely politician were past; perhaps he was tired of the new politics, so different from the era when a tiger shoot and a feast seemed to cement relationships between royalty and heads of state. Perhaps his vanity came into it too, for he was aware he was no longer a dominant voice. In any event, in 1935 the Maharaja of Bikaner turned his back on the federal solution. It was his personal volte-face that turned many other princes against it too

There were less personal reasons for the Chamber of Princes to want to keep its distance from the new Government of India Act. The main one was the bullying of the INC Nehru and others were all for the Congress Party to rule the Indian provinces, but they did not want a federal structure that was designed, as the Act said explicitly, 'to hold India to the Empire'. Realising the princely states had to agree in order for federation to work, they now bullied the princes to veto it. In May 1937, Nehru threatened: 'There is a great deal of talk of independence of the States and of their special treaties. But the thing that is going to count in the future is the treaty that the people of India make with others. The Act will *go* [my italics] inevitably with all its hundreds of sections and its special powers and its federation. I would ask the Princes to consider this matter from this point of view and not rush in where wiser people fear to tread.'[6]

This threat was not to be underestimated, because the Congress Party had just swept to power in seven provinces and researchers calculated it would perform equally well in federal elections for an all-India assembly. Moreover, some of the provincial governments were already in dispute with their princely neighbours over tax and borders; the ancient privileges were in danger.

It is no wonder, then, that many of the COP decided to opt out of the Act or sit on their hands. The stand-off persisted during three and a half years of fruitless negotiation with the India Office. Meanwhile, the provincial governments were allowed to get on with their work. And then, in 1939, the Second World War broke out. Lord Linlithgow committed the Indian population of 400 million to the conflict without asking any of them, a sure sign he had no doubts where power still lay. Soon after, Indian provincial government was withdrawn and India returned to the sort of direct rule from Britain it had not known since before 1919.

On the outbreak of war Ganga Singh, who now held the rank of full general in the British Army, offered to go to the front. When told that age stood in his way, the Maharaja's reply was true to form: *No Rajput is too old to fight at the age of 60.*[7] In 1941 he and his grandson, Karni Singh, went on active service to the Middle East but he returned within a year suffering with terminal cancer. Among many well-wishers who wrote to him was Queen Mary, widow of King George V: 'Do not forget your old friend, Mary.' His last words were typical of his life of conscientious service to the state of Bikaner: *Get me the Bhakra Dam file.*[8] He died in February 1943, aged 62.

At the start of the war the size of the British Indian Army was under 200,000, of which half were Hindu and one-third Muslim. By the end of the war its size had grown to a colossal two and a half million. Set against it was another Indian army of perhaps 80,000 troops called the Indian National Army, who fought alongside the Japanese. Many had been prisoners of war captured during the Japanese offensive of 1942 and released with the assurance they would be fighting for Indian independence.

The Maharaja was succeeded by his son from his first marriage, Sadul Singh, whose brief reign lasted for the most painful period in the history of the state. This was the six years leading to the demise of the kingdom when nearly all the princely states were absorbed into the Union of an independent India in 1949. At the time of the great Maharaja's death it was apparent to most Indians and most British too that the British Raj would not long outlive the war. Indeed, in 1942 the British government had sent Sir Stafford Cripps to India to offer India independence after the war, with the proviso that no part of the country would be forced to join the new nation. In return, all Indian parties were invited to join a government of national unity under the Viceroy until the end of the war. The INC refused the second part of this offer and began a violent 'Quit India' campaign of civil disobedience. It was ruthlessly suppressed and Congress leaders were imprisoned for the duration of the war. It was also apparent the Congress Party and the Muslim League could not share power. Already Jinnah was talking about a new Muslim state called Pakistan, an acronym from *P* of the Punjab, *A* from the Afghan Frontier, *K* from the Kashmir and *istan* from Baluchistan; it also included Sind, and Bengal in the East, all where Muslims predominated.

At the end of the war in 1945, the Viceroy Lord Wavell brought together Gandhi, Jinnah and the Congress leadership to plan the future. They could not agree. The British government was aware it no longer had the troops, money and willpower to coerce a restive India, and when the Labour Party came to power that summer it determined to exit as soon as possible. The next year, in the baking heat of Calcutta in August, a spate of communal violence broke out that made partition the only answer.

When Lord Mountbatten became the last Viceroy in February 1947 he decided on a reckless strategy. He put an arbitrary date on British withdrawal in the hope this deadline would force Hindus and Muslims to come to an agreement. His hope was in vain. On 16 August India was partitioned between Hindus and Muslims in the midst of terrible communal strife. Over the next few months five million Hindus and Sikhs were forced to move from the west Punjab into India and 5.5 million Muslims trekked in the other direction into Pakistan. It was yet another of the 20th century's ethnic cleansings. The new state of India was born at midnight on the 15th. It was, said the first Prime Minister Jawaharlal Nehru in his radio broadcast that night, the redeeming of a pledge, 'a tryst with destiny'. Pakistan had declared independence the previous day. On 30 January 1948 a Hindu zealot assassinated Mahatma Gandhi, hateful of his attempts to reconcile Hindus with Muslims.

By this time the Indian princes were isolated, a price they paid for standing aloof from the 1935 Government of India Act. After intimidation and threats, very nearly all of the states, 552 in number, were persuaded to accede to – 'accede to' being a euphemism used at the time, but more accurate is 'integrate into' – the new India. The two largest princedoms at first refused. Hyderabad joined India after the new Indian Army forced it to do so and the territory of Kashmir is still disputed today between India and Pakistan. Maharaja Sadul Singh took Bikaner into India only after he had threatened to join Pakistan unless the partition boundary through the Punjab was redrawn at the last minute in India's favour, for the source of the essential Gang Canal water lay in the area of Ferozepur which would have gone to Pakistan. Mountbatten agreed, thereby adding to Pakistan's sense of injustice.

It is a sad irony that the intimidation of the princes stemmed from British royalty because Governor-General Lord Mountbatten, as he became after Independence, was both an expert in arm-twisting and a relative of the Royal Family. At first the princes were allowed privileges and a 'privy purse' sweetened the pill. In January 1950 India ceased to be a Dominion, became a Republic and severed its connection with the British Crown. Prime Minister Indira Gandhi, Nehru's daughter, withdrew the subsidy from the princes in 1971, and today their once-magnificent palaces are open to the tourist industry.

What would the 'majestic Maharaja' have made of this? His son died in 1951, the 22nd and last ruler of the desert kingdom. Towards his end the Maharaja of Bikaner was mocked, but he always represented the ideals of the Chamber of Princes in its early days. He believed in the autonomy of the princely states within an autonomous India within the British Empire, a growing contradiction in the modern age. His greatest moment of glory was signing the Treaty of Versailles, just before Clemenceau himself, and it is impossible to think of another Indian prince who had such a prominent role on the international stage. Were Indian politicians not so pre-occupied at the time with their national ambitions they might well have given him more credit for advancing India's influence on the international stage, particularly in the League of Nations. 'We shall not see his like again', said a senior British official, speaking of a living legend.[9]

A large portrait painting in oils is kept of him in a storeroom at the United Nations in Geneva; in the archive is a coloured photograph showing his signature on the Treaty of Versailles. The Treaty itself has been lost, but the magnificent painting by Sir William Orpen, *The Signing of the Peace Treaty in the Hall of Mirrors, Versailles, 28th June 1919*, hangs in the Imperial War Museum in London. There, standing in the centre, is the 'majestic Maharaja' and this epithet by Lloyd George must be how he is best remembered.

Notes

Prologue: 1919

1. KM Panikkar, *His Highness The Maharaja of Bikaner* (Oxford University Press, London: 1937) p 193, hereafter Panikkar.
2. Margaret MacMillan, *Peacemakers: Six Months That Changed the World* (John Murray, London: 2001) p 52; hereafter MacMillan.
3. MacMillan, p 52.
4. MacMillan, p 52.
5. Edwin Montagu Papers, British Library, BL MSS EUR d523, Vol 3; hereafter Montagu Papers.
6. HWV Temperley, *A History of the Peace Conference in Paris* 6 Vols (Hodder & Stoughton, London: 1920) Vol 1, p 245, hereafter Temperley.
7. *Dictionary of National Biography*, India (1972–4) p 245.
8. Montagu Papers, Vol 3.
9. Montagu Papers, Vol 8.
10. Writing to Chelmsford, 19 June 1919; Montagu Papers, Vol 3.
11. Writing to Chelmsford, 19 June 1919; Montagu Papers, Vol 3.

12. Preface to *The Speeches and Writings of Lord Sinha*
    (GA Natesan & Co, Madras: 1919) p ii; hereafter *Sinha Speeches*.
13. Frances Lloyd George, *The Years That Are Past*
    (Hutchinson, London: 1967) p 148.

1 The Maharaja of Bikaner and the Indian Princes

1. Panikkar, p 3.
2. Panikkar, p 16.
3. Panikkar, p 16.
4. Panikkar, p 20.
5. Letter from India Office, quoted by Panikkar, p 22.
6. Panikkar, pp 23–4.
7. LS Rathore, *The Regal Patriot* (Roli Books, New Delhi: 2007) p 15, hereafter Rathore.
8. Panikkar, p 56.
9. Panikkar, p 55.
10. Lawrence James, *Raj, The Making of British India* (Abacus, London: 1997) p 333, hereafter James.
11. Naveen Patnaik, *A Desert Kingdom: the Rajputs of Bikaner* (Weidenfeld and Nicolson, London: 1990) p 26, hereafter Patnaik.
12. Panikkar, p 42.
13. Panikkar, p 47.
14. Rathore, p 172.
15. Rathore, p 34.
16. Sir Walter Lawrence, 'An Appreciation' in Panikkar, p 393.
17. Rathore, p 115.
18. Panikkar, p 365.
19. Rathore, p 174.

20. ADC's Day Book, Archival Research Centre, Lallgarh Palace.
21. Patnaik, p 39.
22. Rathore, p 175.
23. Patnaik, p 37.
24. Pannikar, p 52.
25. Pannikar, p 73.
26. Rathore, p 32.
27. Rathore, p 174.
28. Rathore, p 33.
29. Kenneth Rose, *King George V* (London: 1983) p 352.
30. SD Waley, *Edwin Montagu: A Memoir and an Account of his Visits to India* (Asia Publishing House, Bombay: 1964) p 321, hereafter Waley.
31. David Cannadine, *Ornamentalism, How the British Saw their Empire* (Penguin, London: 2002) p 51.
32. Pannikar, p 131.
33. Pannikar, p 140.
34. Pannikar, p 144.

2 The Indian Army in the First World War

1. Pannikar, pp 150–1.
2. James, p 339.
3. Hugh Tinker, 'From British Army to Indian Army', *Indo-British Review*, Vol 16 (1989) p 3, hereafter Tinker.
4. K Subrahmanyam, 'Indian Armed Forces: Its Ethos and Traditions', *Indo-British Review*, Vol 16 (1989) p 129.
5. Philip Mason, *A Matter of Honour. An Account of the Indian Army, its Officers and Men* (Holt, Rinehart, New York: 1964) p 414, hereafter Mason.
6. Mason, p 443 (both quotes).
7. Tinker, p 1.

8. Tinker, p 4; Lt Gen S K Sinha, 'The Indian Army: Before and After Independence', *Indo-British Review*, Vol 16 (1989) p 178, hereafter Sinha.

9. Sinha, p 178.

10. Mason, p 413.

11. James, p 447.

12. Mason, p 436.

13. Mason, p 437.

14. David Fromkin, *A Peace to End all Peace: Creating the Modern Middle East, 1914 – 1922* (Penguin, London: 1991) p 326.

15. Fromkin, *A Peace to End all Peace*, pp 369–70.

3 SP Sinha and the Indian National Congress

1. John Grigg, *Lloyd George, War Leader 1916–1918* (Penguin Books, London: 2003) p 62, hereafter Grigg.

2. Grigg, p 63.

3. One of the Articles of Faith: www.brahmosamaj.org.

4. *Sinha Speeches*, Preface, p xii.

5. *Sinha Speeches*, Preface, p xiii.

6. Rose, *King George V*, p 64.

7. Barbara and Thomas Metcalf, *A Concise History of India* (Cambridge; New York: 2002) p 137.

8. James, p 354.

9. James, p 354.

10. *Sinha Speeches*, Preface, p xxi.

11. *Sinha Speeches*, pp 47–55.

4 The Imperial War Cabinet and Conference, March–May 1917

1. Grigg, p 61.

2. David Lloyd George, *War Memoirs* (Nicholson and Watson, London: 1936) Vol 1, p 1034.
3. David Lloyd George, *Memoirs of the Peace Conference* (Yale University Press, New Haven: 1939) pp 126–7.
4. Pannikar, pp 174–6.
5. Panikkar, pp 174–6.
6. Rose, *King George V*, p 348.
7. Rose, *King George V*, p 348.
8. Rose, *King George V*, p 350.
9. Ganga Singh, *India's Imperial Partnership. The Speeches of the Maharaja of Bikaner During his Visit to England as One of the Indian delegates to the Imperial War Cabinet and the Imperial War Conference, 1917* (The Times, London: 1917) pp 13 and 25, hereafter Singh.
10. Singh, p 22.
11. *Sinha Speeches*, Preface, p xxxii.
12. *Sinha Speeches*, Preface, p xxxi.
13. Pannikar, pp 186–90.

5 The Montagu-Chelmsford Reforms

1. Waley, pp 84–5.
2. Grigg, p 185.
3. Grigg, p 183.
4. James, p 458.
5. E S Montagu, *A Study in Indian Politics* (GA Natesan & Co, Madras: 1925) p 78.
6. James, p 458.
7. Montagu, *A Study in Indian Politics*, pp 22–3.
8. James, p 460 (both quotes).
9. Montagu Papers, Vol 3.
10. James, p 458.
11. James, p 458.

12. James, p 458.
13. Ian Copland, *The Princes of India in the End Game of Empire, 1917–1947* (Cambridge University Press, Cambridge: 1997) p 40, hereafter Copland.
14. An aphorism attributed to the English cleric Charles Caleb Cotton (1780–1832).
15. *Sinha Speeches*, Preface, p xxxiv.
16. Pannikar, p 190.
17. Grigg, p 544.

6 The Call to Peace

1. Archival Research Centre, Bikaner, File 5579.
2. Archival Research Centre, Bikaner, File 5579.
3. Panikkar, p 195.
4. Waley, pp 192–3.
5. Waley, pp 192–3.
6. MacMillan, p 54.
7. WH Hughes, *Policies and Potentates* (Sydney: 1950) p 244.
8. MacMillan, p 53.
9. MacMillan, p 53.
10. MacMillan, p 65.
11. MacMillan, p 51.
12. Temperley, Vol 6, p 343.
13. MacMillan, p 53.
14. Lloyd George, *Memoirs of the Peace Conference*, p 126.
15. Letters from Montagu to Chelmsford, Montagu Papers, Vol 3.

7 The Paris Peace Conference – India and The League of Nations

1. MacMillan, p 95.

2. Viscount Cecil, *The Great Experiment* (Jonathan Cape, London: 1941) p 85.
3. MacMillan, p 95.
4. Lloyd George, *Memoirs of the Peace Conference*, p 98.
5. Lloyd George, *Memoirs of the Peace Conference*, p 127.
6. Waley, p 197.
7. Temperley, Vol 2, p 26.
8. MacMillan, p 95.
9. MacMillan, p 104; Cecil, *The Great Experiment*, p 87.
10. Cecil, *The Great Experiment*, p 86
11. Pannikar, p 202.
12. Pannikar, pp 198–200.
13. Pannikar, p 202.
14. Pannikar, p 202.
15. Pannikar, p 202.
16. Waley, p 197.
17. Lloyd George Papers, Beaverbrook Library, F/89/2/29 Feb 1919.
18. Patnaik, p 37.
19. Lord Sinha's Peace Conference Papers. Minutes of British Empire delegation Meetings. British Library GS EUR F281/43.
20. Maharaja Ganga Singh Trust: File 7243.
21. Cecil, *The Great Experiment*, p 88.
22. Hughes, *Policies and Potentates*, p 245.
23. David Hunter Miller, *Drafting of the Covenant*, Vol I (GP Putnam, New York: 1928) pp 267–9.
24. Hunter Miller, *Drafting of the Covenant*, Vol 2, pp 324–5.
25. Hughes, *Policies and Potentates*, p 245.
26. Hunter Miller, *Drafting of the Covenant*, Vol 1, pp 461–6.

27. Hunter Miller, *Drafting of the Covenant*, Vol 1, pp 461–6.
28. Lord Sinha's Peace Conference Papers. Minutes of Covenant Committee BL EUR F281/41.
29. MacMillan, p 328.
30. Lord Sinha's Peace Conference Papers. Minutes of British Empire delegation Meetings. British Library SS EUR F281/7.
31. *Sinha Speeches*, Preface, p xxv.
32. Pannikar, p 207.
33. Temperley, Vol 2, p 37.
34. Temperley, Vol 2, p 38.

8 The Paris Peace Conference – India and the Ottoman Empire

1. MacMillan, p 414.
2. Maharaja Ganga Singh Trust: File 6423 Note 19.
3. Maharaja Ganga Singh Trust: File 5582.
4. MacMillan, p 407.
5. Temperley, Vol 6, p 23.
6. Temperley, Vol 6, footnote on p 24.
7. MacMillan, p 391.
8. James, p 469.
9. Montagu, *A Study in Indian Polity*, p 59.
10. Lord Sinha's Peace Conference Papers. Minutes of British Empire delegation Meetings. British Library SS EUR F281/102.
11. H Nicolson, *Peacemaking 1919* (Constable, London: 1944) p 340.
12. Montagu to Lord Willingdon Letters 1918–1919, Montagu Papers, Vol 16.
13. Panikkar, p 204.

14. Panikkar, p 206.
15. Montagu to Lord Willingdon Letters 1918–1919, Montagu Papers, Vol 16.
16. MacMillan, p 447.
17. Letter from Montagu to Chelmsford, 28 May 1919, Montagu Papers, Vol 3.
18. Maharaja Ganga Singh Trust: File 5582.
19. Maharaja Ganga Singh Trust: File 5582.
20. AG Grant and Harold Temperley, *Europe in the Nineteenth and Twentieth Centuries* (Longman, London: 1971), quoted by Rathore, p 83.
21. Rathore, p 83.
22. Maharaja Ganga Singh Trust; File 7243.
23. Montagu to Lord Willingdon Letters 1918–1919, Montagu Papers, Vol 16.

9 Reform and Revolt, 1919–24

1. Appendix to Singh.
2. Waley, pp 209–10.
3. James, p 460.
4. Waley, p 214.
5. James, p 468.
6. These were the official figures. James, p 473.
7. Maharaja Ganga Singh Trust: File 5582.
8. Montagu/Chelmsford Letters, Montagu Papers, Vol 3.
9. Chelmsford/Montagu Letters, Montagu Papers, Vol 8.
10. Montagu/Willingdon Letters, Montagu Papers, Vol 16.
11. Fromkin, *A Peace to End All Peace*, p 431.
12. Montagu/Willingdon, 20 May 1920, Montagu Papers, Vol 16.
13. MacMillan, p 460.
14. MacMillan, p 447.

15. Montagu, *A Study in Indian Politics*, p 74.
16. Peter Rowland, *David Lloyd George* (London: 1975) p 580.
17. Rowland, *David Lloyd George*, p 580.
18. MacMillan, p 464.
19. Alan Palmer, *The Decline and Fall of the Ottoman Empire* (J Murray, London: 1992) p 265.

10 Towards Independence: the Rise of the Congress Party

1. James, p 535.

11 Towards Independence: Bikaner and the Fall of the Princes

1. Pannikar, p 334.
2. Copland, p 48.
3. Rathore, p 138.
4. Copland, p 79.
5. Copland, footnote, p 155.
6. Copland, p 156.
7. Patnaik, p 40.
8. Rathore, p 176.
9. Copland, p 193.

Chronology

YEAR	AGE	THE LIFE
1880		Ganga Singh Bikaner born.
1885	5	Indian National Congress (INC) founded.
1887	7	Ganga Singh succeeds to throne as Maharaja of Bikaner.
1897	17	Bikaner marries first wife, Princess of Pratapgarh.
1898	18	Bikaner assumes royal power.
1899	19	Lord Curzon becomes Viceroy.
1900	20	Bikaner on active service with British Army in China to suppress Boxer Uprising.
1902	22	Bikaner attends Coronation of Edward VII; is made ADC to Prince of Wales. Son and heir, Prince Sadul Singh, born.

YEAR	HISTORY	CULTURE
1880	Transvaal Republic declares independence from Britain.	Fyodor Dostoevsky, *The Brothers Karamazov*.
1885	General Charles Gordon killed in fall of Khartoum to the Mahdi.	Guy de Maupassant, *Bel Ami*.
1887	Britain's Queen Victoria celebrates Golden Jubilee.	Arthur Conan Doyle, *A Study in Scarlet*.
1897	Crete proclaims union with Greece: Ottoman Empire declares war, defeated in Thessaly; Peace of Constantinople.	H G Wells, *The Invisible Man*. Edmond Rostand, *Cyrano de Bergerac*.
1898	Horatio H Kitchener defeats Mahdists at Omdurman.	Oscar Wilde, *The Ballad of Reading Gaol*.
1899	Anglo-Egyptian Sudan Convention. Second Boer War begins.	Rudyard Kipling, *Stalky and Co*.
1900	Second Boer War: Mafeking relieved, Johannesburg and Pretoria captured.	Sigmund Freud, *The Interpretation of Dreams*. Joseph Conrad, *Lord Jim*.
1902	Treaty of Vereeniging ends Boer War. First meeting of Committee of Imperial Defence.	Arthur Conan Doyle, *The Hound of the Baskervilles*. Maxim Gorki, *Lower Depths*.

YEAR	AGE	THE LIFE
1905	25	Curzon attempts to partition Bengal: leads to riots, rise of first 'home rule' nationalists like Bal Tilak; Curzon resigns.
		Prince of Wales (future King George V) visits Bikaner.
1906	26	Congress splits over issue of 'extremism': All India Muslim League formed following year.
1909	29	Satyendra Sinha appointed to Viceroy's Executive Council – first Indian to share in government of India.
1910	30	Bikaner attends Coronation of King George V; arranges Imperial Durbar for King's visit to India.
1911	31	Attempt to assassinate Viceroy Hardinge. Partition of Bengal repealed.
1914	34	India joins First World War, fighting for British Empire: Bikaner serves in Europe. British Indian Army active in France and Mesopotamia.

YEAR	HISTORY	CULTURE
1905	Russo-Japanese War: Port Arthur surrenders to Japanese. 'Bloody Sunday': police break-up Russian demonstration, by Tsar Nicholas II issues the 'October Manifesto'.	E M Forster, *Where Angels Fear to Tread.* Edith Wharton, *House of Mirth.*
1906	British ultimatum forces Turkey to cede Sinai Peninsula to Egypt.	John Galsworthy, *A Man of Property.* First jukebox invented.
1909	Britain's Edward VII makes state visits to Berlin and Rome.	H G Wells, *Tono-Bungay.*
1910	South Africa becomes Dominion within British Empire with Louis Botha as Premier.	E M Forster, *Howard's End.* Karl May, *Winnetou.*
1911	German gunboat *Panther* arrives in Agadir: triggers international crisis. Italy declares war on Turkey.	D H Lawrence, *The White Peacock.* Saki (H H Munro), *The Chronicles of Clovis.*
1914	Archduke Franz Ferdinand of Austria-Hungary and wife assassinated in Sarajevo. First World War begins: Battles of Mons, the Marne and First Ypres.	James Joyce, *Dubliners.* Theodore Dreiser, *The Titan.* Film: Charlie Chaplin in *Making a Living.*

YEAR	AGE	THE LIFE
1915	35	SP Sinha elected President of Indian National Congress.
		German-Turkish plot to stir up insurrection against British suppressed.
		Bikaner fights in Egypt with *Ganga Risala* before returning to India.
1916	36	Congress re-united at Lucknow session of INC. All India Home Rule League for Independence within Empire formed.
		Mohandas Gandhi returns to India from London. Bikaner elected Secretary to Princes' Conference.
1917	37	Bikaner and Sinha invited to London to join Imperial War Cabinet and Conference; Bikaner given Freedom of City of London, writes Rome Note on future of India. Edwin Montagu appointed Secretary of State for India, begins work with Viceroy Chelmsford on proposals for Government of India Bill.

YEAR	HISTORY	CULTURE
1915	First World War: Battles of Neuve Chapelle and Loos, 'Shells Scandal', Gallipoli campaign; Germans execute British nurse Edith Cavell in Brussels for harbouring British prisoners. Germans sink British liner *Lusitania*, killing 1,198.	Joseph Conrad, *Victory*. John Buchan, *The Thirty-Nine Steps*. Ezra Pound, *Cathay*. Film: *The Birth of a Nation*.
1916	First World War: Battles of Verdun and the Somme. US President Woodrow Wilson issues Peace Note to belligerents in European war. David Lloyd George becomes British Prime Minister.	Lionel Curtis, *The Commonwealth of Nations*. James Joyce, *Portrait of an Artist as a Young Man*. Film: *Intolerance*.
1917	First World War: Battle of Passchendaele (Third Ypres); British and Commonwealth forces take Jerusalem; USA declares war on Germany; China declares war on Germany and Russia. February Revolution in Russia. Balfour Declaration favouring establishment of national home for Jewish People in Palestine.	P G Wodehouse, *The Man With Two Left Feet*. T S Eliot, *Prufrock and Other Observations*. Leon Feuchtwanger, *Jud Suess*. Film: *Easy Street*.

YEAR	AGE	THE LIFE
1918	38	Mrs Annie Besant elected President of INC.
		War ends.
		Widespread influenza epidemic; economic slide begins.
		Rise of Khilafat Movement.
		Sinha attends another Imperial War Cabinet and Conference.
		Bikaner meets Montagu in India to discuss formation of Chamber of Princes.
		Nov: Bikaner summoned to London for final Imperial War Cabinet and Conference.
1919	39	Government of India Act passed.
		Rowlatt Acts passed to quell civil disobedience.
		Amritsar massacre ordered by General Dyer.
		Gandhi calls for *swaraj* and *satyagraha*.
		Motilal Nehru becomes President of INC.
		Sinha given title of Lord Sinha of Raipur: appointed Under Secretary of State for India, pilots Government of India Act through House of Lords.
		Jan: Sinha and Bikaner appointed Plenipotentiaries at Paris Peace Conference.
		Feb/Mar: Bikaner argues successfully for India's inclusion in League of Nations.
		May/ Jun: Bikaner and Sinha argue for better treatment of Ottoman Empire.
		Jun: Bikaner signs Treaty of Versailles, returns to India.

YEAR	HISTORY	CULTURE
1918	First World War: Peace Treaty of Brest-Litovsk signed between Russia and Central Powers; German Spring offensives on Western Front fail. Allied offensives on Western Front have German army in full retreat; Armistice signed between Allies and Germany; German Fleet surrenders. Ex-Tsar Nicholas II and family executed Kaiser Wilhelm II of Germany abdicates.	Alexander Blok, *The Twelve*. Gerald Manley Hopkins, *Poems*. Luigi Pirandello, *Six Characters in Search of an Author*. Bela Bartok, *Bluebeard's Castle*. Giacomo Puccini, *Il Trittico*. Gustav Cassel, *Theory of Social Economy*. Oskar Kokoshka, *Friends and Saxonian Landscape*. Edvard Munch, *Bathing Man*.
1919	Communist Revolt in Berlin. Benito Mussolini founds Fascist movement in Italy. Britain and France authorise resumption of commercial relations with Germany. British-Persian agreement at Tehran to preserve integrity of Persia. Irish War of Independence begins. US Senate vetoes ratification of Versailles Treaty leaving US outside League of Nations.	Bauhaus movement founded by Walter Gropius. Wassily Kandinsky, *Dreamy Improvisation*. Paul Klee, *Dream Birds*. Thomas Hardy, *Collected Poems*. Herman Hesse, *Demian*. George Bernard Shaw, *Heartbreak House*. Eugene D'Albert, *Revolutionshochzeit*. Edward Elgar, Concerto in E Minor for Cello. Manuel de Falla, *The Three-Cornered Hat*. Film: *The Cabinet of Dr Caligari*.

YEAR	AGE	THE LIFE
1920	40	Renewed war in Afghanistan.
		Gandhi continues call for *satyagraha*: Congress members leave government posts; Jawaharlal Nehru organises peasant *kisans*; Congress now committed to *swaraj*; the Nehrus imprisoned.
1921	41	Bikaner appointed Chancellor of Chamber of Princes; receives King George V on his second visit to India.
1922	42	'Tiger' Clemenceau visits Bikaner.
		Chauri Chaura incident: *Swaraj* campaign out of control; Gandhi ends *satyagraha*, retires temporarily to village life.
1924	44	Bikaner represents Ruling Princes at League of Nations.
1926	46	Bikaner resigns as Chancellor of Chamber of Princes.
1927	47	Gang Canal in Bikaner opens.
1928	48	Simon Commission sent to India.
		Dec: Nehrus demand Dominion status and withdrawal of British from India at Congress AGM; Muhammad Ali Jinnah demands constitutional separation for Muslims.

YEAR	HISTORY	CULTURE
1920	League of Nations comes into existence. Bolsheviks win Russian Civil War. Adolf Hitler announces his 25-point programme in Munich.	F Scott Fitzgerald, *This Side of Paradise.* Franz Kafka, *The Country Doctor.* Katherine Mansfield, *Bliss.*
1921	Irish Free State established. Peace treaty signed between Russia and Germany. Washington Naval Treaty signed.	John Dos Passos, *Three Soldiers.* Salzburg Festival established.
1922	Chanak crisis. League of Nations Council approves British Mandate in Palestine.	F Scott Fitzgerald, *The Beautiful and Damned.* BBC founded: first radio broadcasts.
1924	German Nazi Party enters Reichstag with 32 seats for first time after elections.	King George V makes first royal radio broadcast, opening British Empire Exhibition at Wembley.
1926	Germany admitted to League of Nations; Spain leaves as result. Imperial Conference in London decides Britain and Dominions are autonomous communities, equal in status.	A A Milne, *Winnie the Pooh.* Ernest Hemingway, *The Sun Also Rises.* Film: *The General.*
1927	Inter-Allied military control of Germany ends.	Film: *The Jazz Singer.*
1928	Transjordan becomes self-governing under British Mandate. Kellogg-Briand Pact outlawing war and providing for peaceful settlement of disputes signed.	D H Lawrence, *Lady Chatterley's Lover.* Aldous Huxley, *Point Counterpoint.*

YEAR	AGE	THE LIFE
1929	49	Viceroy Irwin promises Dominion status for India, calls for Round Table Conference in London. Congress rejects invitation, calls for new round of civil disobedience.
1930	50	26 Jan: 'Independence Day'; another *satyagraha* for *swaraj* called; Gandhi leads 'salt march'.
		Bikaner represents Ruling Princes at League of Nations, Imperial Conference and Round Table discussions on future of India in London: proposes federation between princely states and British Indian provinces.
1931	51	Gandhi meets with Viceroy Irwin: calls off *satyagraha* and agrees to another Round Table Conference in London; Congress decides on another boycott.
1935	55	Bikaner opposes new Government of India Act that concedes provincial self-rule but requires federation at national level to be agreed by Chamber of Princes.
		INC decides to contest elections: forms Congress Party; wins control of five provinces, is largest party in two others, but will not share power.
		Jinnah believes united India only possible if rights of Muslims protected; many more Muslims join his Muslim League.

YEAR	HISTORY	CULTURE
1929	Fascists win single-party elections in Italy.	Ernest Hemingway, *A Farewell to Arms*.
	Germany accepts Young Plan at Reparations Conference in the Hague: Allies agree to evacuate Rhineland.	Erich Maria Remarque, *All Quiet on the Western Front*.
		Noel Coward, *Bittersweet*.
	Wall Street Crash.	
1930	Britain, France, Italy, Japan and US sign London Naval Treaty regulating naval expansion.	T S Eliot, *Ash Wednesday*.
		W H Auden, *Poems*.
	Nazi Party gains 107 seats in German Reichstag.	Noel Coward, *Private Lives*.
	Constantinople's name changed to Istanbul.	
1931	Austrian Credit-Anstalt bankruptcy begins Central Europe's financial collapse.	Noel Coward, *Cavalcade*.
		William Faulkner, *Sanctuary*.
	National Government formed in Britain.	Robert Frost, *Collected Poems*.
		Films: *Dracula. Little Caesar*.
	Britain abandons Gold Standard.	
1935	Saarland incorporated into Germany following plebiscite.	T S Eliot, *Murder in the Cathedral*.
	British King George V's Silver Jubilee.	Emlyn Williams, *Night Must Fall*.
		Ivy Compton-Burnett, *A House and its Head*.
	Hoare-Laval Pact.	
	Hitler announces anti-Jewish 'Nuremberg Laws'; Swastika becomes Germany's official flag.	Films: *The 39 Steps. Top Hat*.
	League of Nations imposes sanctions against Italy following invasion of Abyssinia.	

YEAR	AGE	THE LIFE
1936	56	Princes cannot agree, but provincial self-rule goes ahead until suspended by war in 1939. Congress now joint ruler of India.
1937	57	Maharaja of Bikaner celebrates Golden Jubilee; attends Coronation of King George VI in London.
1939	59	Viceroy Linlithgow commits India to war without consultation.
1940	60	Jinnah calls for separate state for Muslims called Pakistan.
1941	61	British Indian Army numbers 400,000: half Hindu, one-third Muslim. Emergency Powers Act passed to prevent civil insurrection.

YEAR	HISTORY	CULTURE
1936	German troops occupy Rhineland violating Treaty of Versailles.	J M Keynes, *General Theory of Employment, Interest and Money.*
	British King George V dies: succeeded by Edward VIII, who abdicates at end of year to marry Wallis Simpson; succeeded by George VI.	A J Ayer, *Language, Truth and Logic.*
		Berlin Olympics.
		Films: *Modern Times. Camille. The Petrified Forest. Things to Come.*
	Franco mutiny in Morocco and throughout Spain starting Spanish Civil War.	BBC begins world's first television transmission service.
1937	UK Royal Commission on Palestine recommends partition into British and Arab areas and Jewish state.	George Orwell, *The Road to Wigan Pier.*
		Films: *Snow White and the Seven Dwarfs. Elephant Boy.*
1939	Second World War begins: Germany invades Poland; Britain and France declare war; Soviets invade Finland.	John Steinbeck, *The Grapes of Wrath.*
		Films: *The Wizard of Oz. Gunga Din.*
1940	Second World War:	Graham Greene, *The Power and the Glory.*
	Battle of Britain.	Film: *Rebecca.*
	Italy invades Greece.	
1941	Second World War:	Noel Coward, *Blithe Spirit.*
	Germany invades USSR.	Films: *Citizen Kane. Dumbo. The Maltese Falcon.*
	Japan attacks Pearl Harbor, invades the Philippines.	

YEAR	AGE	THE LIFE
1942	62	Sir Stafford Cripps visits India on behalf of British government: offers independence after war, provided no community forced to join; talks break down; Gandhi retaliates with 'Quit India' campaign of civil disobedience; British suppress it ruthlessly; Congress leaders imprisoned until end of war.
1943	63	Feb: Maharaja of Bikaner dies.
1945		War ends.
		Viceroy Wavell brings together Gandhi, Jinnah and Congress leadership to plan future: Hindus, Muslims cannot agree on power sharing.
		Jul: Labour Government wins power in Britain, determined to get out of India.
1946		Aug: 'Great Calcutta Killing': religious war breaks out between Hindus and Muslims that makes partition only solution.
1947		Lord Mountbatten becomes last Viceroy: decides Britain will leave Subcontinent by August, after partition between Hindus and Muslims.
		14 Aug: Pakistan declares independence; India becomes independent night after.
		Indian Princes forced to give up independence and join India or Pakistan. Kashmir and Hyderabad refuse, leading to war. Bikaner joins India.

YEAR	HISTORY	CULTURE
1942	Second World War: Singapore surrenders to Japanese: Japanese invade Burma. US surrender in Philippines. Dolittle Raid: US bombs Tokyo. US invasion of Guadalcanal turns Japanese tide.	Enid Blyton publishes first 'Famous Five' book, *Five on a Treasure Island.* Albert Camus, *The Outsider.* T S Eliot, *Little Gidding.* Films; *Casablanca. The Jungle Book.*
1943	Second World War: Allies demand unconditional surrender from Germany and Japan at Casablanca Conference.	Jean-Paul Sartre, *Being and Nothingness.* Films: *For Whom the Bell Tolls. Bataan.*
1945	Second World War: British troops liberate Burma. VE Day: 8 May. US drops atomic bombs on Hiroshima and Nagasaki: Japan surrenders to Allies.	Jean-Paul Sartre, *The Age of Reason.* Evelyn Waugh, *Brideshead Revisited.* Films: *Brief Encounter. The Way to the Stars.*
1946	UN General Assembly opens in London. Churchill declares Stalin has lowered 'Iron Curtain' across Europe, signalling formal start of Cold War.	Bertrand Russell, *History of Western Philosophy.* Eugene O'Neill, *The Iceman Cometh.* Films: *Great Expectations. It's a Wonderful Life.*
1947	'Truman Doctrine' pledges to support 'free peoples resisting subjugation by armed minorities or outside pressures'. US Secretary of State George C Marshall calls for relief aid to Europe. New Japanese constitution renounces use of war.	Edinburgh Festival is founded. Albert Camus, *The Plague.* Anne Frank, *The Diary of Anne Frank.* Tennessee Williams, *A Streetcar Named Desire.* Films: *Monsieur Verdoux. Black Narcissus.*

YEAR	AGE	THE LIFE
1950		India ceases to be Dominion: ends allegiance to British Crown, becomes Republic.

YEAR	HISTORY	CULTURE
1950	Korean War breaks out.	Ezra Pound, *Seventy Cantos.*
	USSR and China sign 30-year Treaty of Friendship.	Films: *Sunset Boulevard. Kim.*

Further Reading

This is not a subject much has been written about before. I have been able to access three sources of primary material. The first is the collection of papers of the Maharaja of Bikaner in the Archival Research Centre at the Lallgarh Palace in Bikaner, Rajasthan. These will repay greater study than I had time for. The other two collections are in the British Library in London. The first are Lord Sinha's papers of the Peace Conference. I found most interesting the Minutes of the British Empire delegation and the Minutes of the Covenant Committee, though like all official minutes they reveal little of the argument that took place. The second are the Edwin Montagu Letters, exchanged between him, Viceroy Chelmsford and Lord Willingdon, Governor of Bombay at that time. Montagu's letters are entertaining because for a statesman he was indiscreet and effusive.

Biographies of the three Indian Plenipotentiaries are few. There are two Indian biographies of Ganga Singh, Maharaja of Bikaner. Both are hagiographic by British standards and the second adds very little to the first, although it was written 70 years later. The earlier of the two, written in 1937 when the Maharaja was in power, is *His Highness The Maharaja of*

Bikaner by KM Panikkar (Oxford University Press, London: 1937). Panikkar knew the Maharaja well in his later years because he was Foreign Minister for the Maharaja of Patiala as well as being a constitutional historian and barrister. His insights, therefore, are first-hand and his hagiography understandable. His successor as biographer is Professor LS Rathore, whose book *The Regal Patriot* (Roli Books, New Delhi: 2007) does have magnificent photographs. No biography has been written of Satyendra Sinha, though *The Speeches and Writings of Lord Sinha*, with a biographical introduction, was published in Madras in 1919 (GA Natesan & Co, Madras). It is in the British Library. Surprisingly, there is no biography of Edwin Montagu though SD Waley's *Edwin Montagu: A Memoir and an Account of His Visits to India* (Asia Publishing House, Bombay: 1964) is worth reading. It draws heavily on Montagu's letters, mentioned above. There is also an emotional essay written by a Muslim admirer in India and published in 1925, *E. S. Montagu, A Study in Indian Politics* (GA Natesan & Co, Madras). This, too, is in the British Library. All three have entries in the *Dictionary of National Biography*, and both the Maharaja of Bikaner and Lord Sinha are also in the *Indian Dictionary of National Biography*.

For histories of the Peace Conference, Margaret MacMillan's *Peacemakers: Six Months That Changed the World* (John Murray, London: 2001) is a superb read, authoritative but irreverent. I expect most writers in this series have drawn on it. More sober and much heavier, though clearly written, is the six-volume standard work edited by HWV Temperley, who was in Paris at the time: *A History of the Peace Conference* (Hodder & Stoughton: 1920, and OUP: 1969). Another near contemporary history is David Hunter

Miller's *Drafting of the Covenant* (GP Putnam, New York: 1928). Two major British participants whose memoirs I found helpful, if self-serving, were Lloyd George himself, *Memoirs of the Peace Conference* (Yale University Press, New Haven: 1930) and Robert Cecil, *The Great Experiment* (Jonathan Cape, London: 1941) about his role founding the League of Nations. In the last volume of John Grigg's masterly biography, *Lloyd George, War Leader 1916–1918* (Penguin Books, London: 2003), there is valuable information about Edwin Montagu and the Imperial Prime Minister's Cabinet and Conference.

On the British in India during the first half of the 20th century, the most vigorously written and wide-ranging history is by Lawrence James, *Raj, The Making of British India* (Abacus, London: 1997). Also worth reading is *A Concise History of India* by Barbara and Thomas Metcalf (Cambridge University Press: 2002). Philip Mason, who worked for the Indian Civil Service, wrote a most readable book on the British Indian Army, *A Matter of Honour* (Holt, Rinehart, New York: 1964), and for those who want an Indian perspective I recommend a series of essays in the special edition of a now-defunct magazine, the *Indo-British Review*. The essays are 'The Indian Armed Forces; its Ethos and Traditions' by K Subrahmanyam and 'The Indian Army; Before and After Independence' by SK Sinha. Both are in Vol 16, published in Madras in 1989. Ian Copland has contributed an academic analysis of the role of the Indian Princes during these years, *The Princes of India in the End Game of Empire 1917–1947* (Cambridge University Press, Cambridge: 1999) which offers a corrective to the hagiographic biographies of the Maharaja.

Picture Sources

The author and publishers wish to express their thanks to the following sources of illustrative material and/or permission to reproduce it. They will make proper acknowledgements in future editions in the event that any omissions have occurred.

Courtesy of the Maharaja Ganga Singhji Trust, Lallgarh Palace, Bikaner, India and Topham Picturepoint.

Endpapers
The Signing of Peace in the Hall of Mirrors, Versailles, 28th June 1919 by Sir William Orpen (Imperial War Museum: akg-images, London)
Front row: Dr Johannes Bell (Germany) signing with Herr Hermann Müller leaning over him
Middle row (seated, left to right): General Tasker H Bliss, Col E M House, Mr Henry White, Mr Robert Lansing, President Woodrow Wilson (United States); M Georges Clemenceau (France); Mr David Lloyd George, Mr Andrew Bonar Law, Mr Arthur J Balfour, Viscount Milner, Mr G N Barnes (Great Britain); Prince Saionji (Japan)

Back row (left to right): M Eleftherios Venizelos (Greece); Dr Afonso Costa (Portugal); Lord Riddell (British Press); Sir George E Foster (Canada); M Nikola Pašić (Serbia); M Stephen Pichon (France); Col Sir Maurice Hankey, Mr Edwin S Montagu (Great Britain); the Maharajah of Bikaner (India); Signor Vittorio Emanuele Orlando (Italy); M Paul Hymans (Belgium); General Louis Botha (South Africa); Mr W M Hughes (Australia)

Jacket images

(Front): Imperial War Museum: akg Images.
(Back): *Peace Conference at the Quai d'Orsay* by Sir William Orpen (Imperial War Museum: akg Images).
Left to right (seated): Signor Orlando (Italy); Mr Robert Lansing, President Woodrow Wilson (United States); M Georges Clemenceau (France); Mr David Lloyd George, Mr Andrew Bonar Law, Mr Arthur J Balfour (Great Britain); Left to right (standing): M Paul Hymans (Belgium); Mr Eleftherios Venizelos (Greece); The Emir Feisal (The Hashemite Kingdom); Mr W F Massey (New Zealand); General Jan Smuts (South Africa); Col E M House (United States); General Louis Botha (South Africa); Prince Saionji (Japan); Mr W M Hughes (Australia); Sir Robert Borden (Canada); Mr G N Barnes (Great Britain); M Ignacy Paderewski (Poland)

Index

Makers of the Modern World

UK PUBLICATION: November 2008 to December 2010
CLASSIFICATION: Biography/History/
    International Relations
FORMAT: 198 × 128mm
EXTENT: 208pp
ILLUSTRATIONS: 6 photographs plus 4 maps
TERRITORY: world

Chronology of life in context, full index, bibliography innovative layout
with sidebars